Be Italian

Jimmy Angelina & Wyatt Doyle

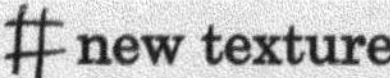

For the Italians.

A New Texture book

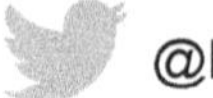 @NewTexture   NewTexture.com    @ThisIsNewTexture

BeItalianBook.com   JimmyAngelina.com

Back cover: **Mercedes Ruehl as Connie Russo, Married to the Mob (1988)**

Signed and numbered oversized hardcover available from **BeItalianBook.com**

To commission or purchase original artwork by Jimmy Angelina,
email **LastColoringBook@gmail.com**

ISBN 978-1-943444-46-5

First New Texture softcover edition: October 2021

First printing

Printed in the United States of America

10 9 8 7 6 5 4 3 2 1

Chico: Well how did you get to be Roscoe W. Chandler?

Abie: Say, how did *you* get to be an Italian?

Chico: Never mind, whose confession is this?

Animal Crackers (1930)

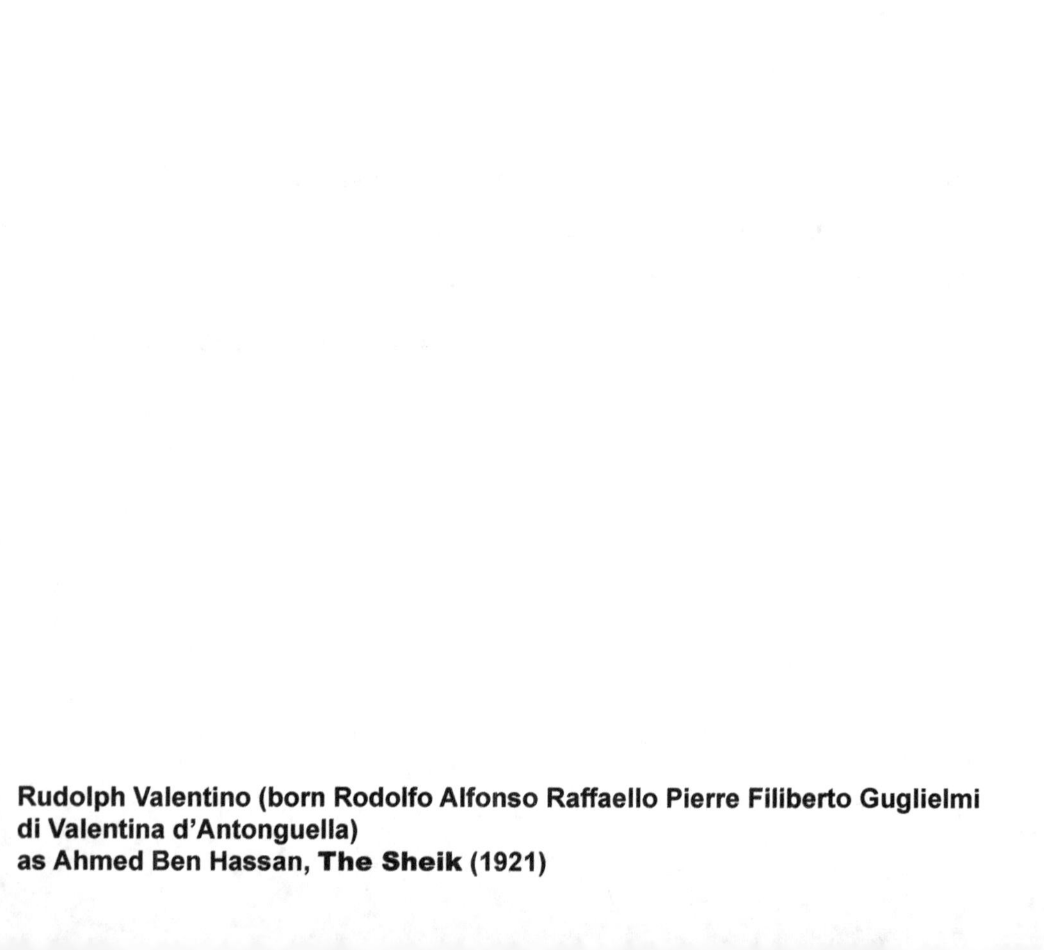

**Rudolph Valentino (born Rodolfo Alfonso Raffaello Pierre Filiberto Guglielmi di Valentina d'Antonguella)
as Ahmed Ben Hassan, The Sheik (1921)**

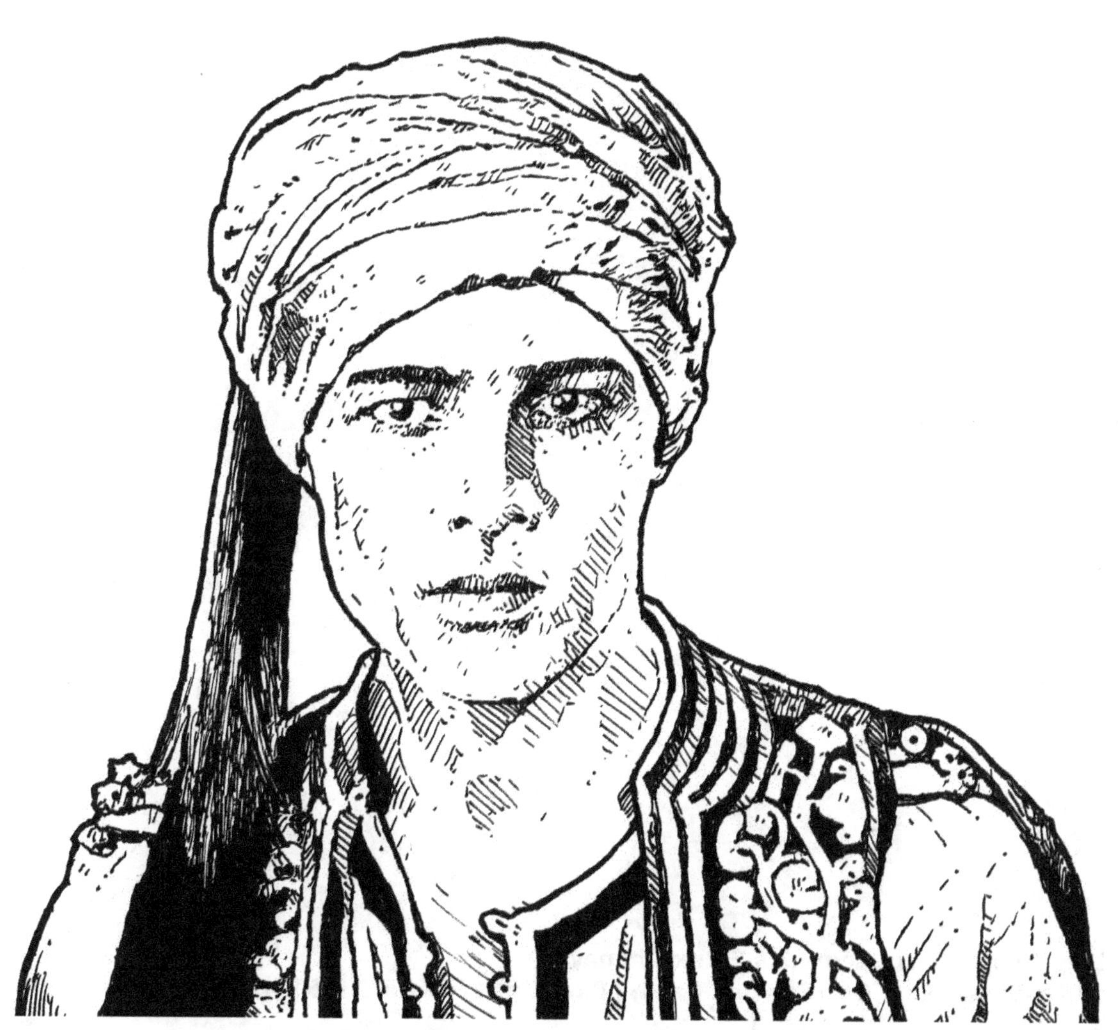

Lon Chaney (born Leonidas Frank Chaney)
as Tony Pantelli, **The Light of Faith [The Light in the Dark]** (1922)

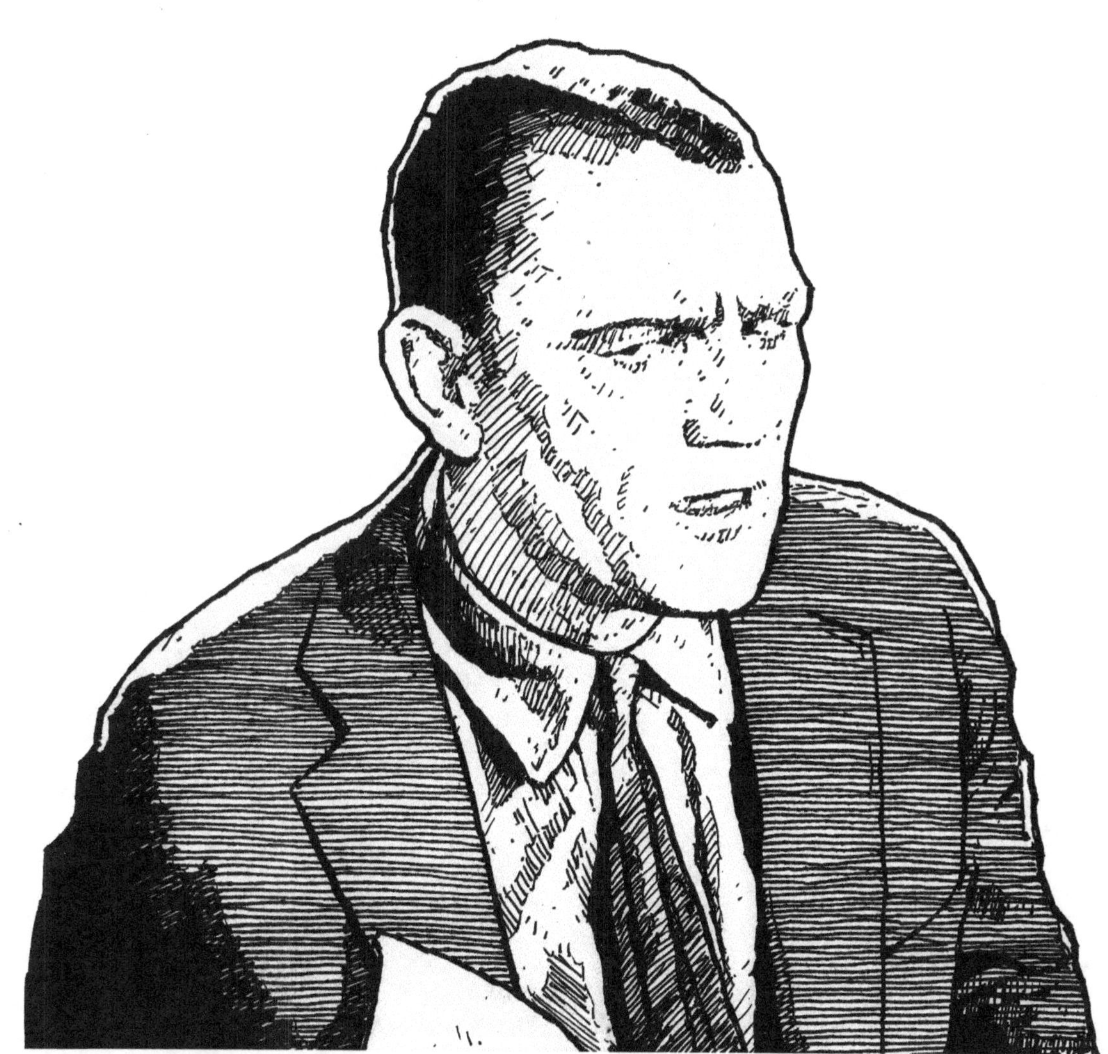

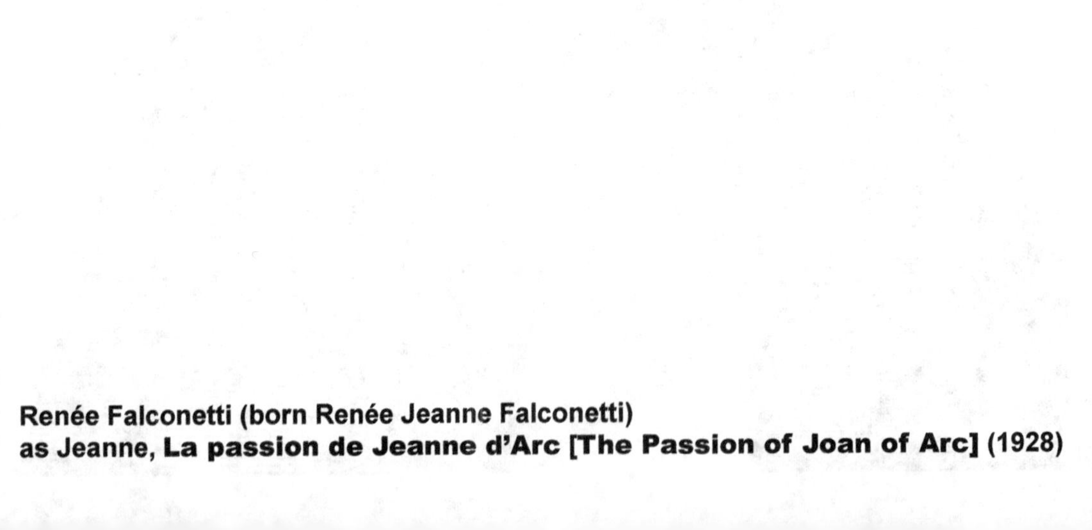

Renée Falconetti (born Renée Jeanne Falconetti)
as Jeanne, **La passion de Jeanne d'Arc [The Passion of Joan of Arc]** (1928)

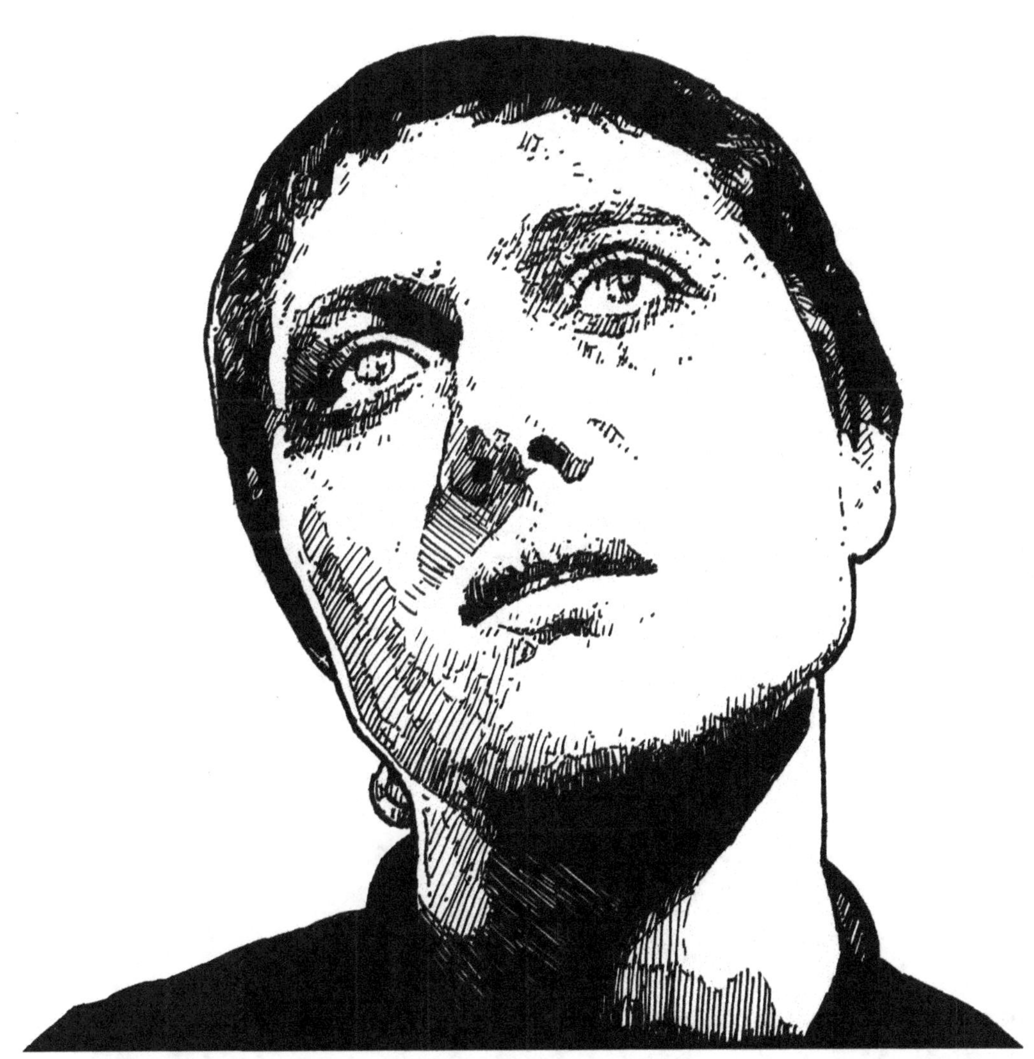

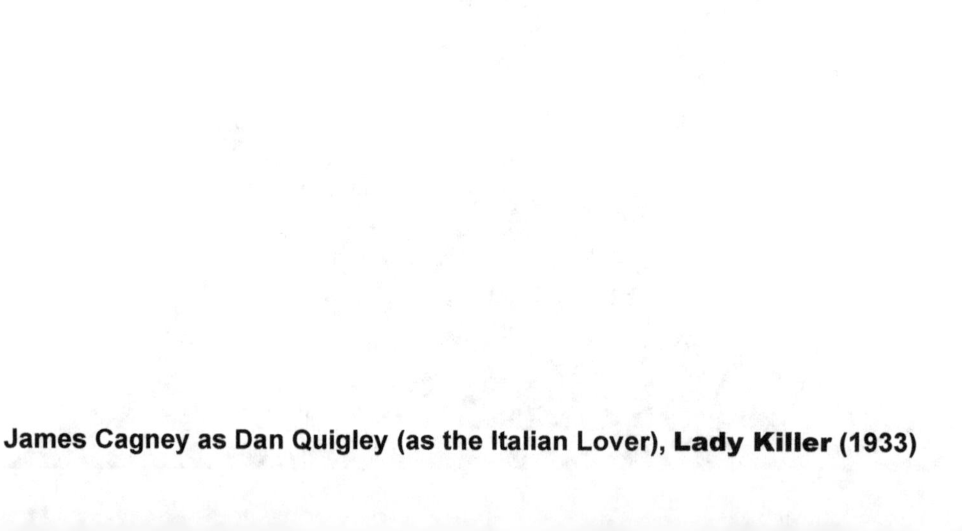

James Cagney as Dan Quigley (as the Italian Lover), **Lady Killer** (1933)

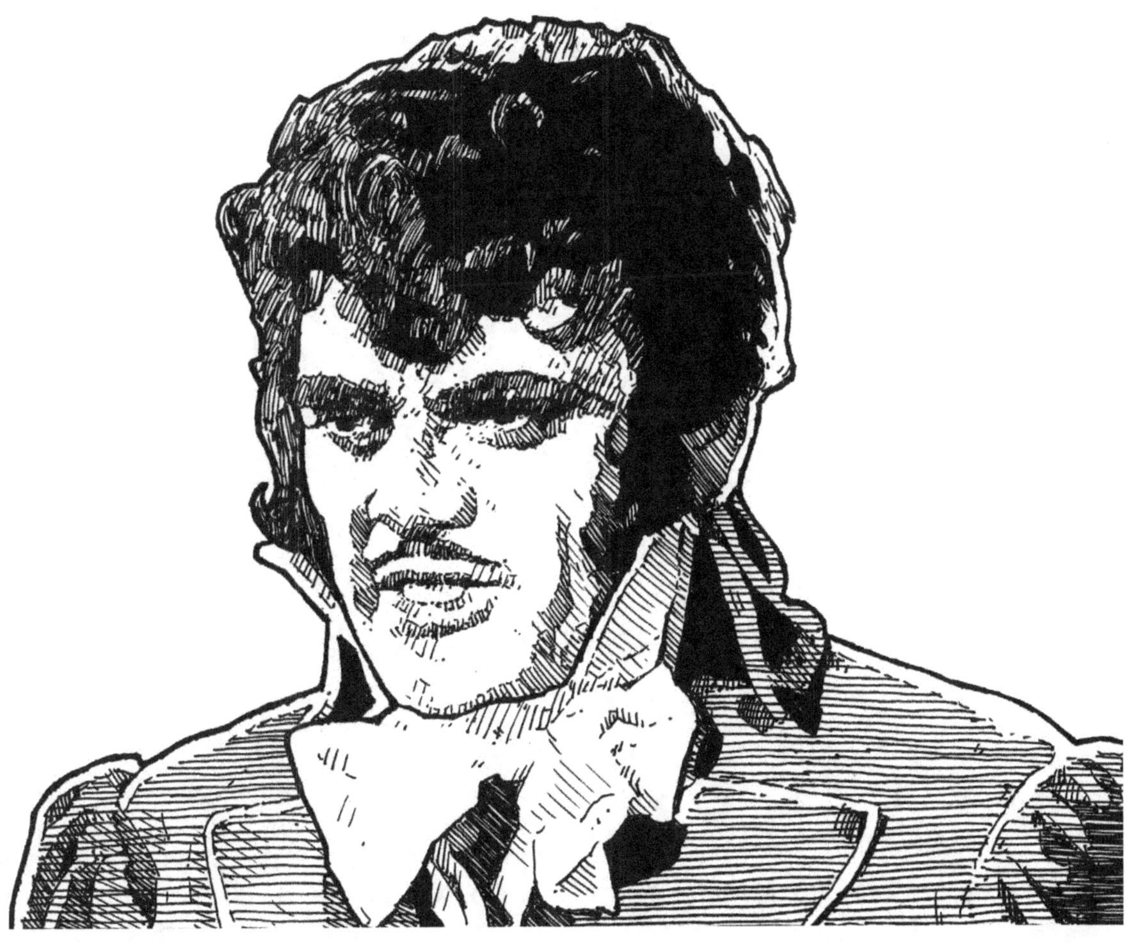

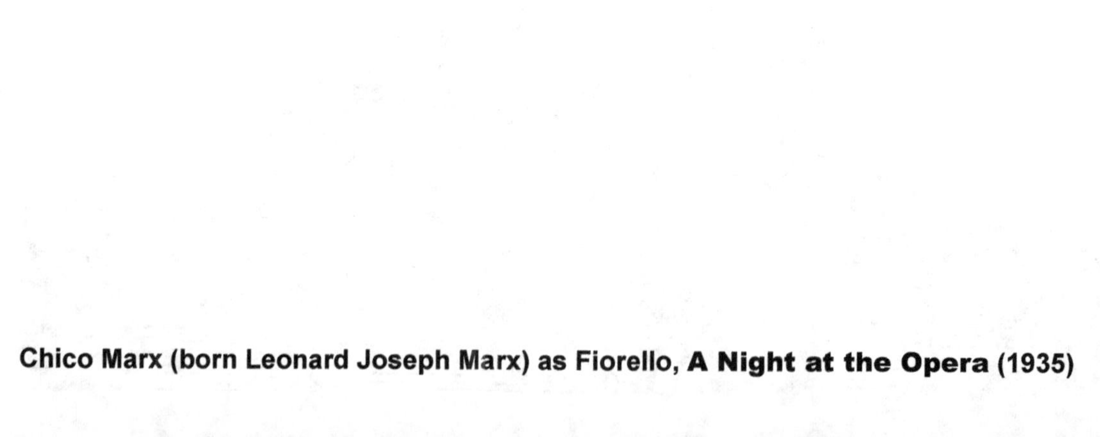

Chico Marx (born Leonard Joseph Marx) as Fiorello, **A Night at the Opera** (1935)

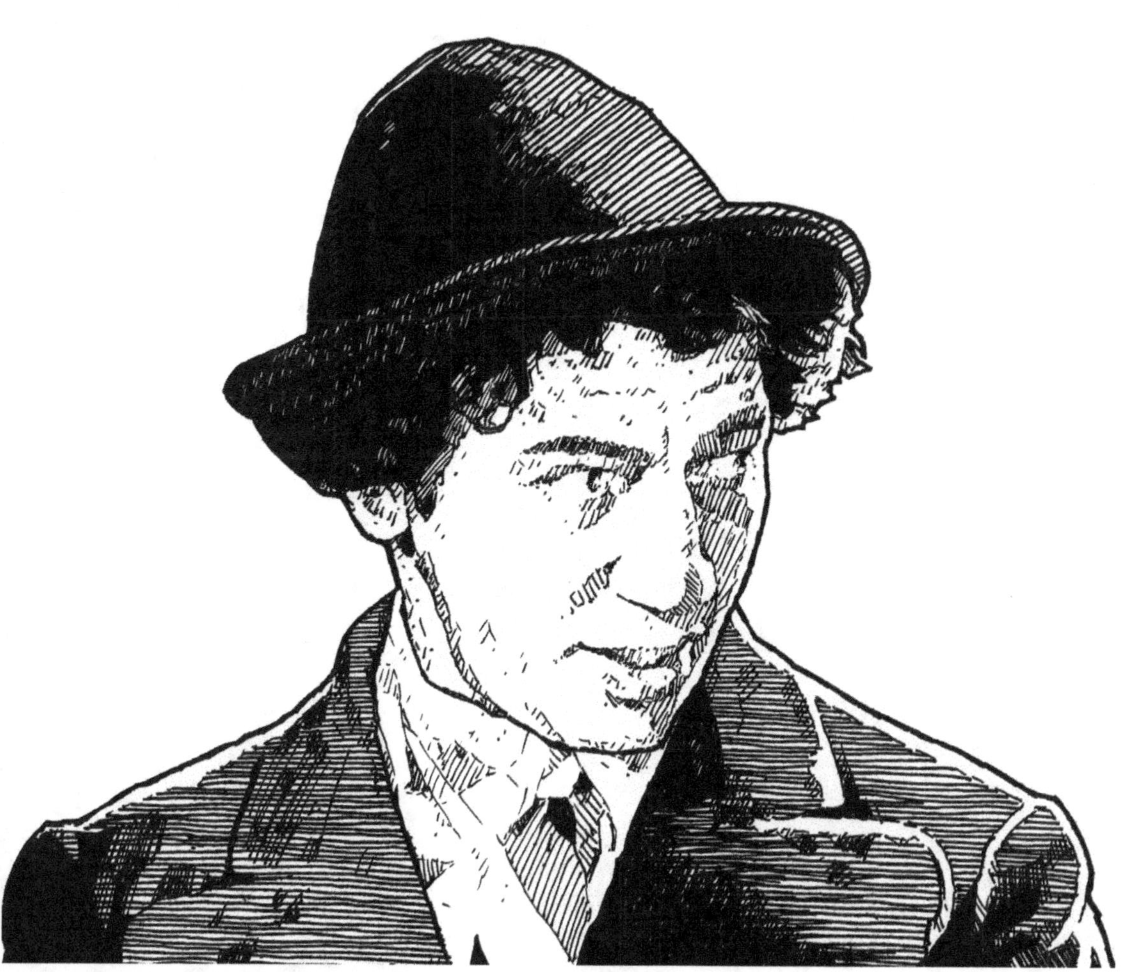

Bela Lugosi (born Béla Ferenc Dezső Blaskó)
as Prince Saliano, **You'll Find Out** (1940)

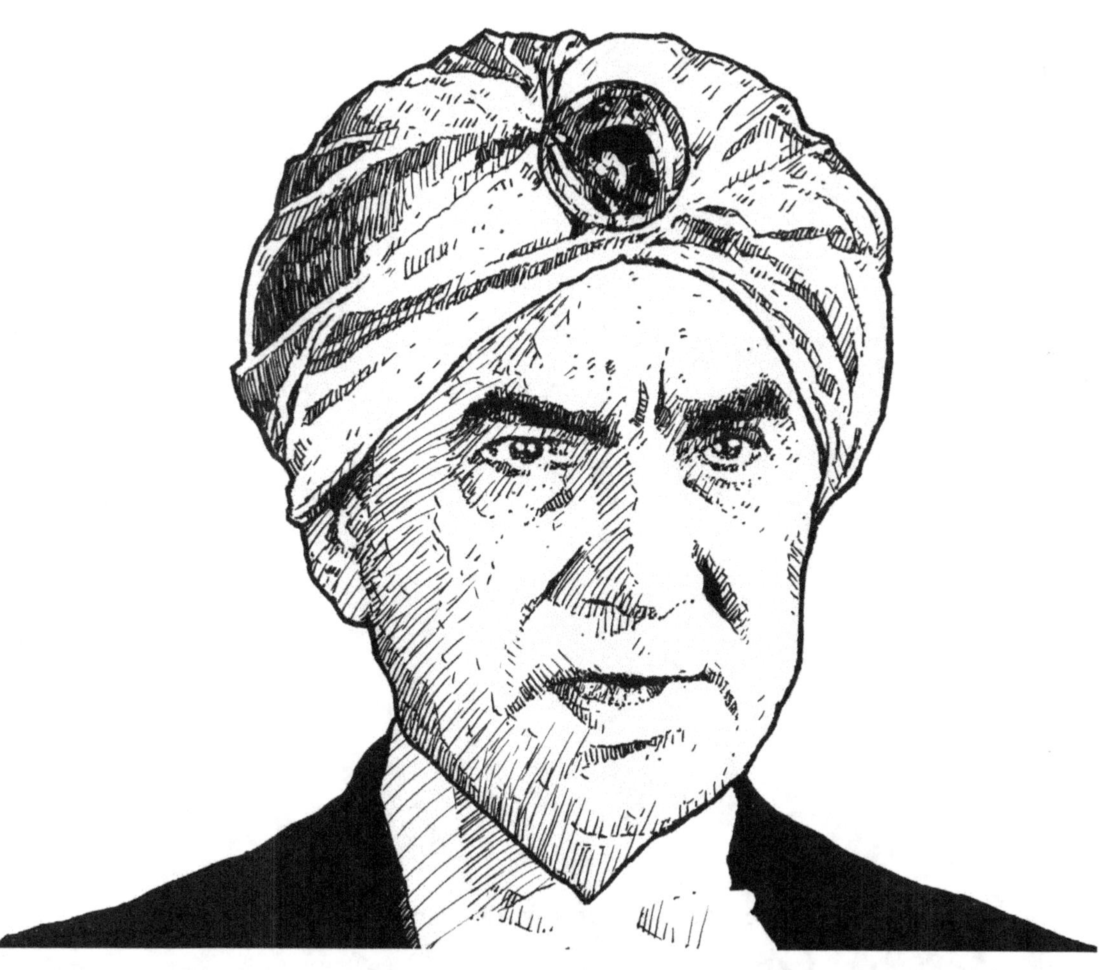

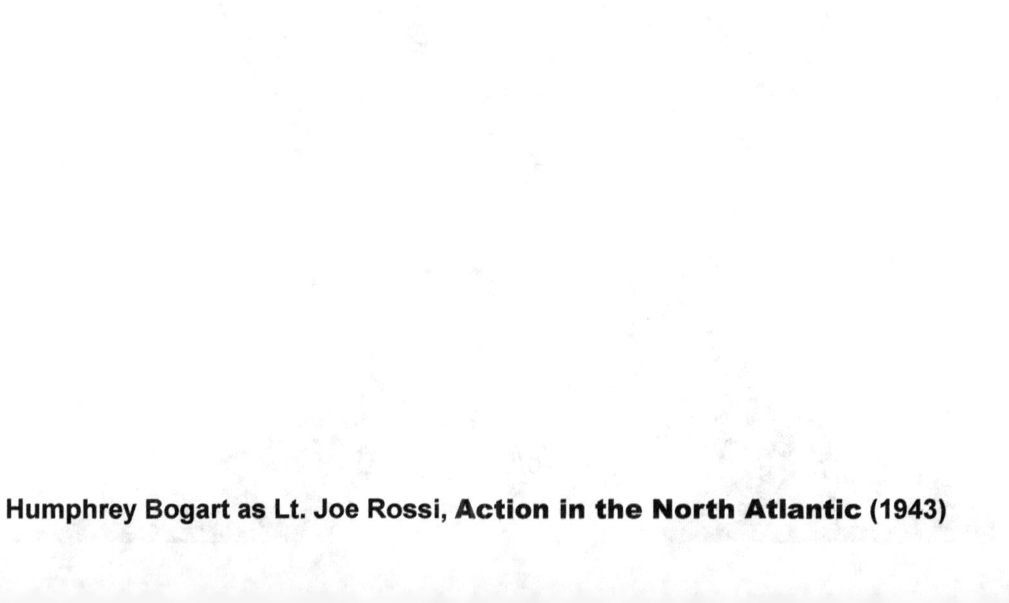

Humphrey Bogart as Lt. Joe Rossi, *Action in the North Atlantic* (1943)

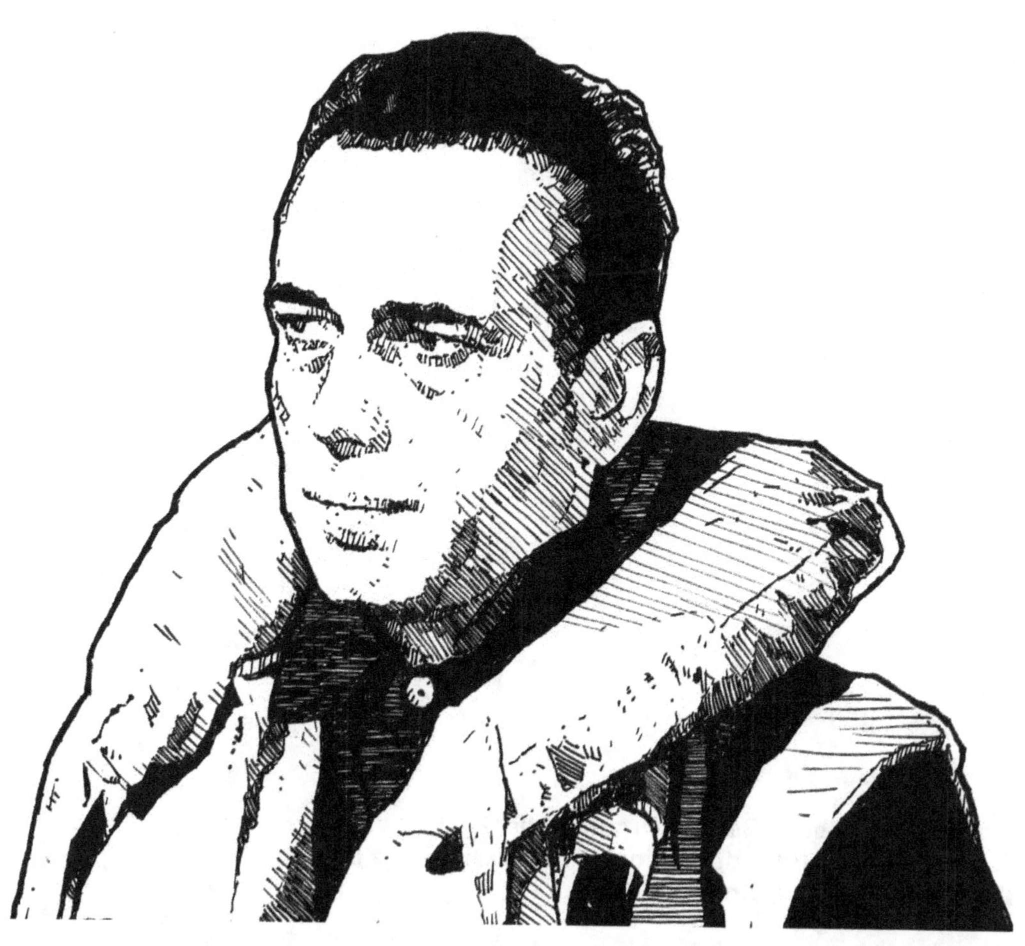

Orson Welles (born George Orson Welles)
as Count Alessandro di Cagliostro (born Giuseppe Balsamo),
Black Magic [Cagliostro] (1949)

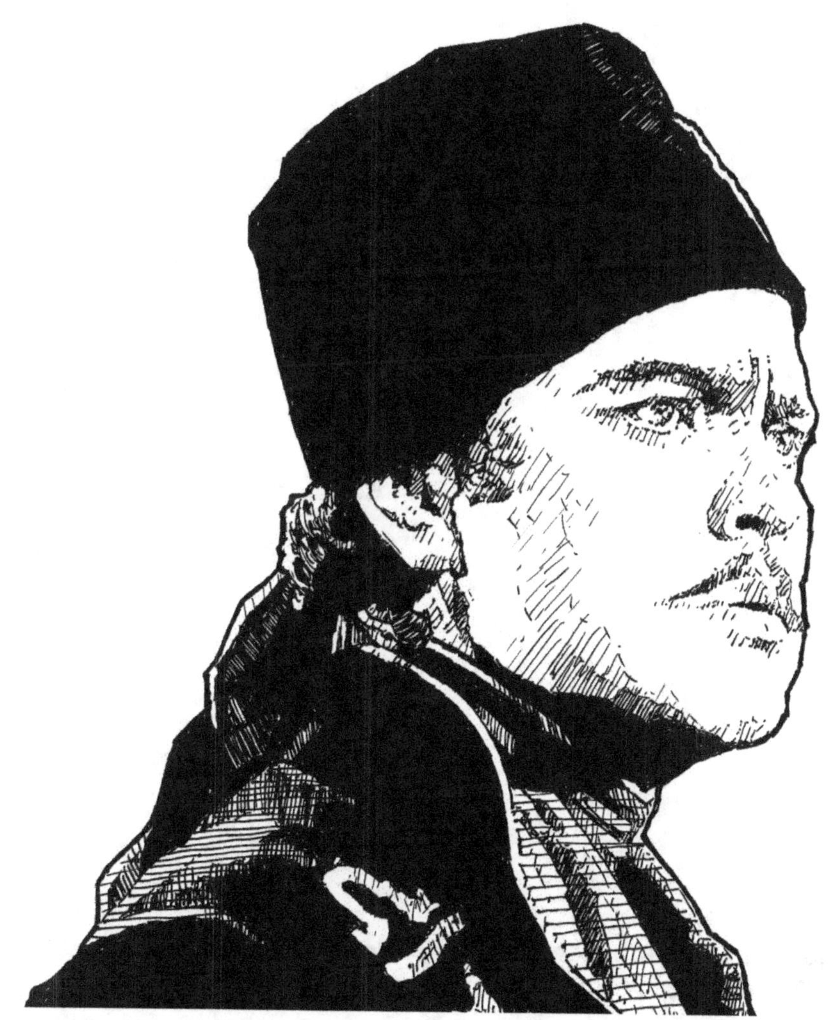

Anthony Quinn (born Manuel Antonio Rodolfo Quinn Oaxaca)
as Zampanò, **La Strada** (1954)

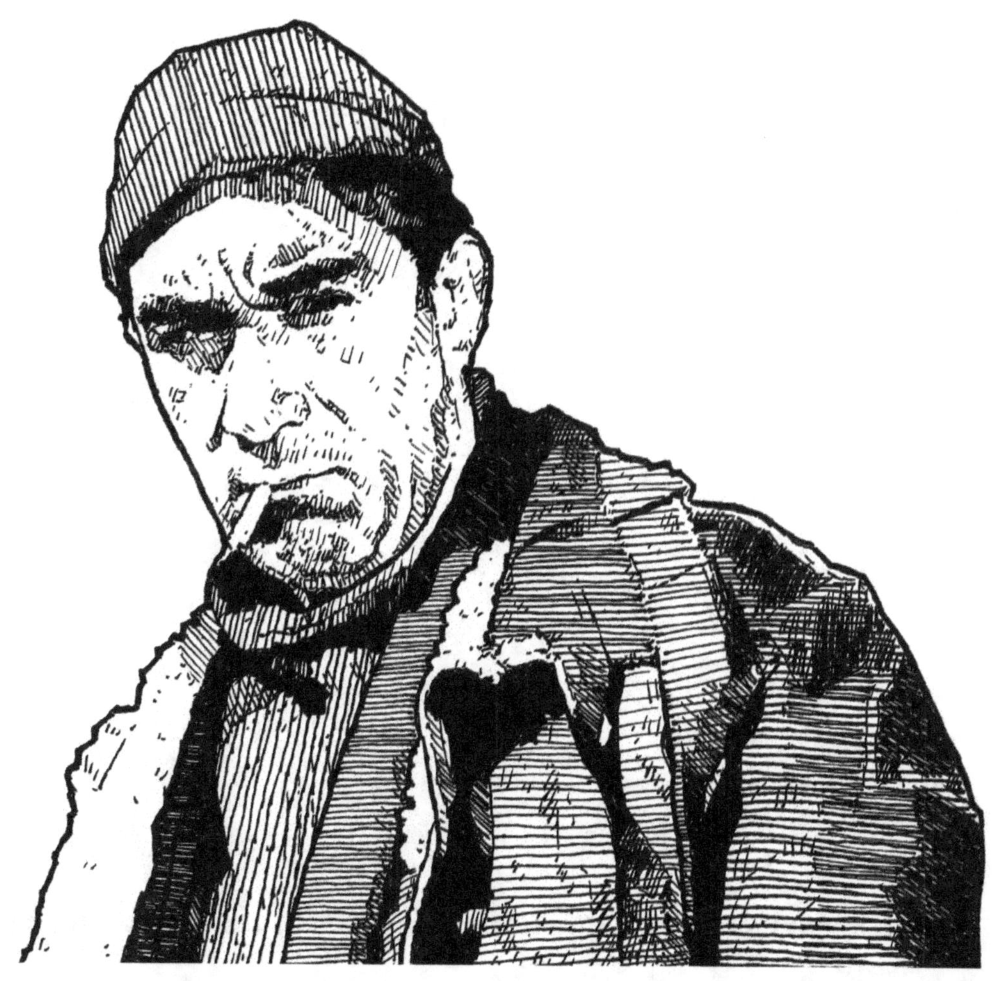

Ernest Borgnine (born Ermes Effron Borgnino) as Stadt, **Violent Saturday** (1955)

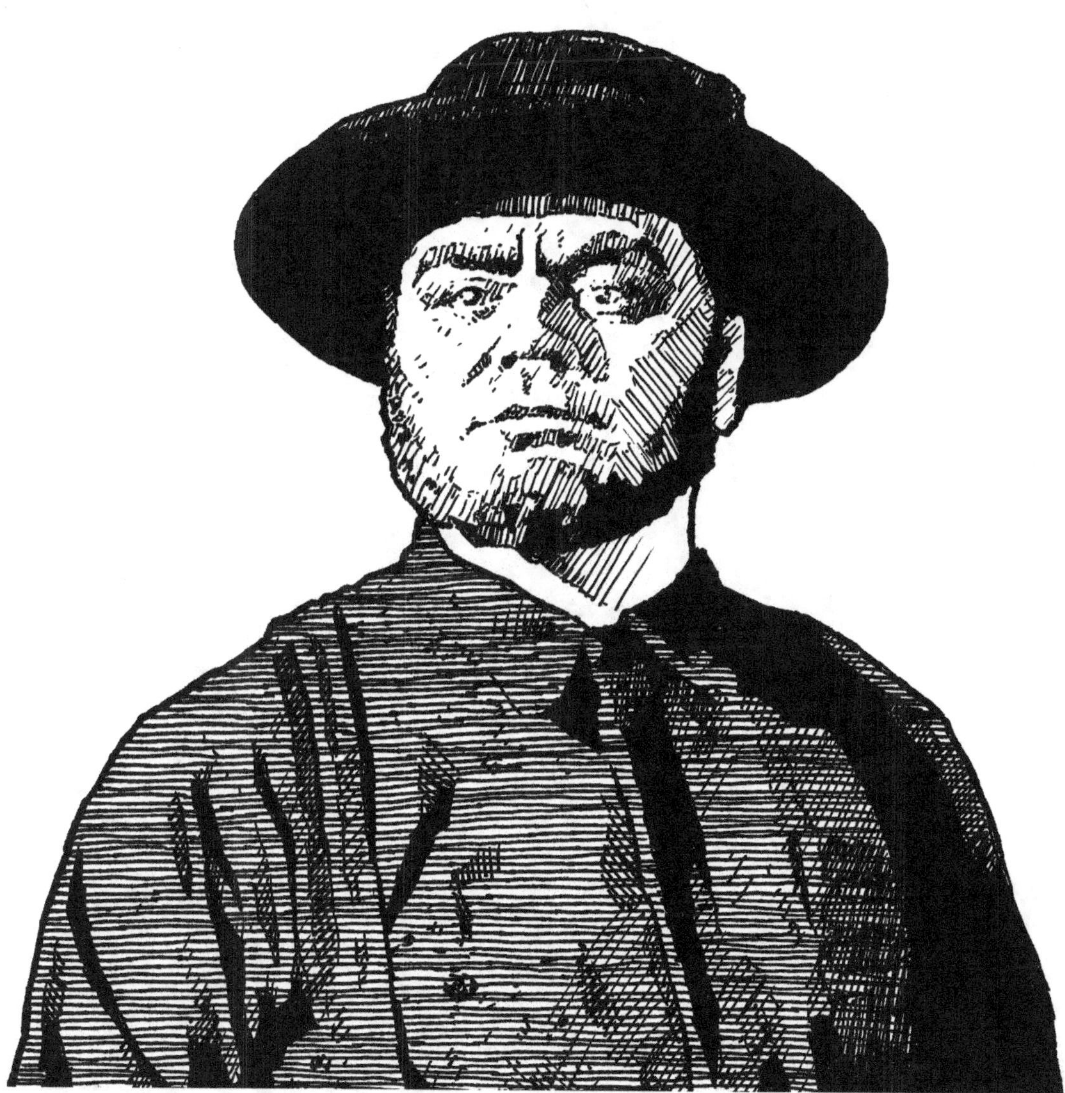

Judy Holliday (born Judith Tuvim) as Emily Rocco, **Full of Life** (1956)

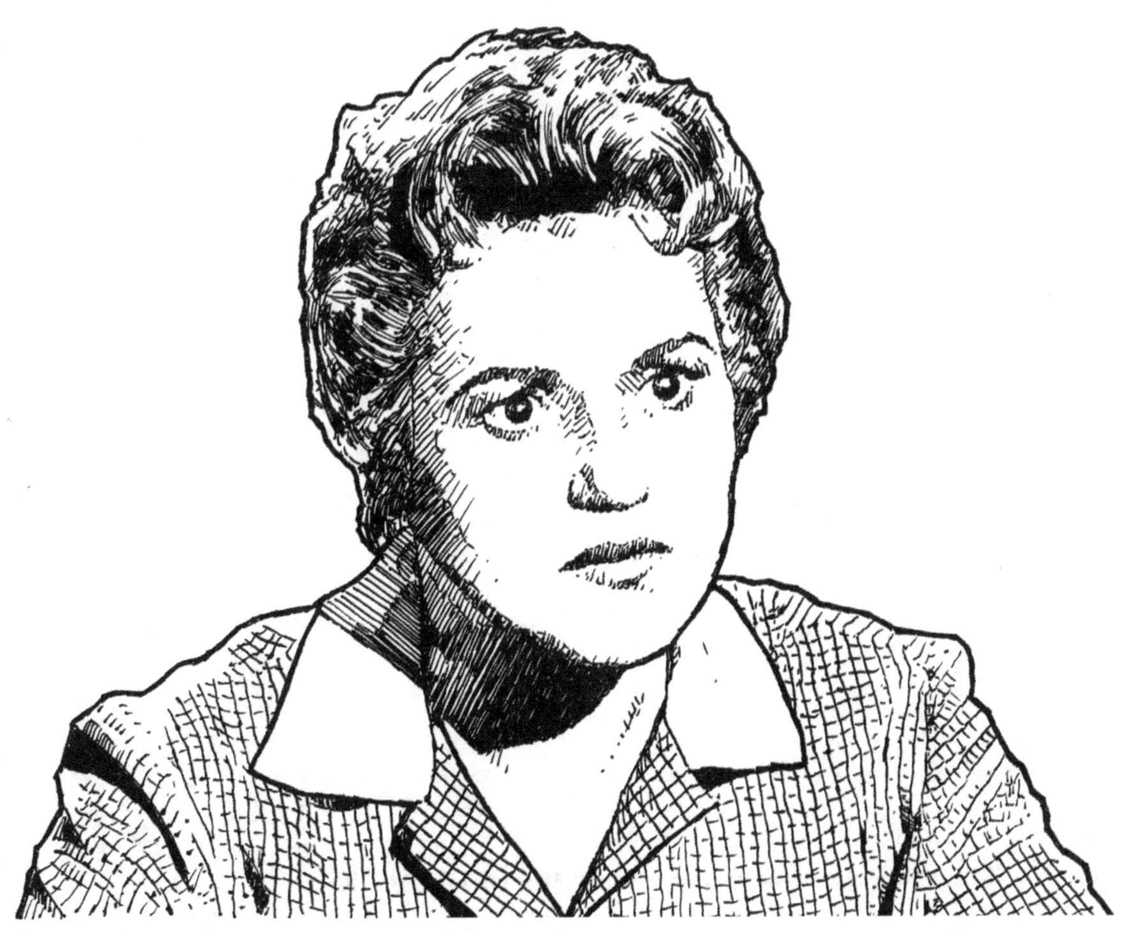

Timothy Carey as Private Maurice Ferol, **Paths of Glory** (1957)

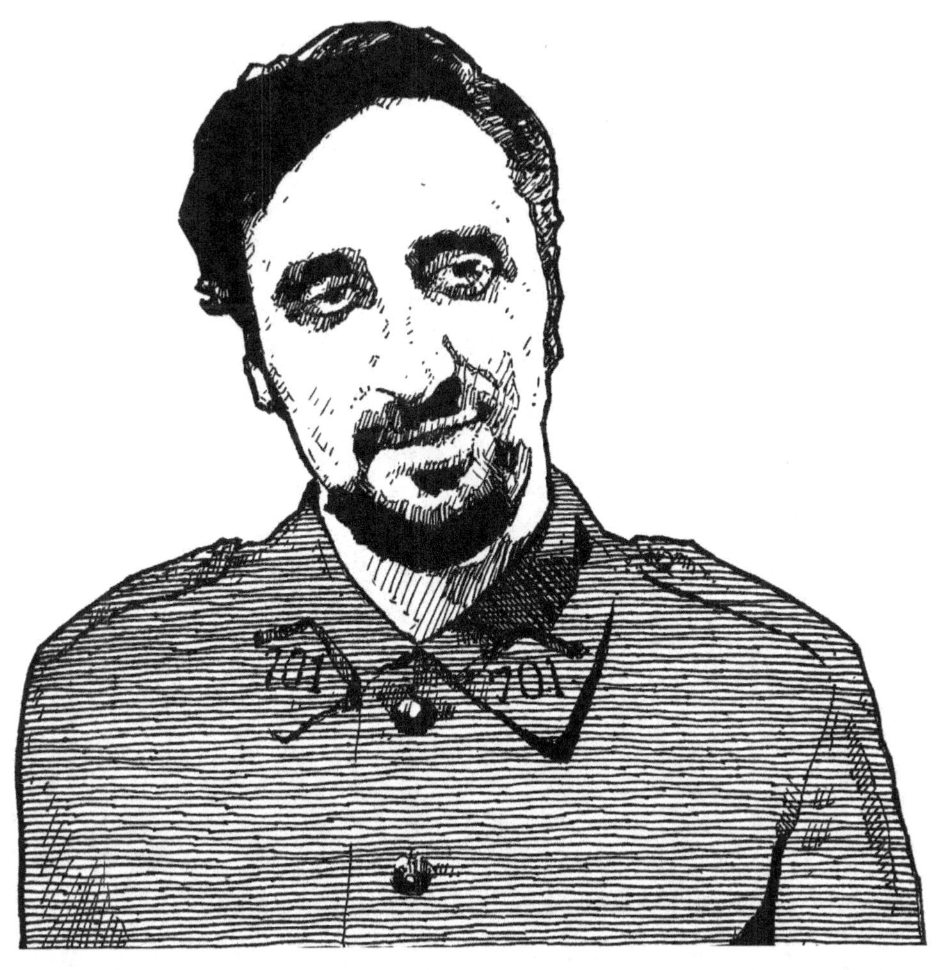

Frank Sinatra as Phil Hirsh, Some Came Running (1958)

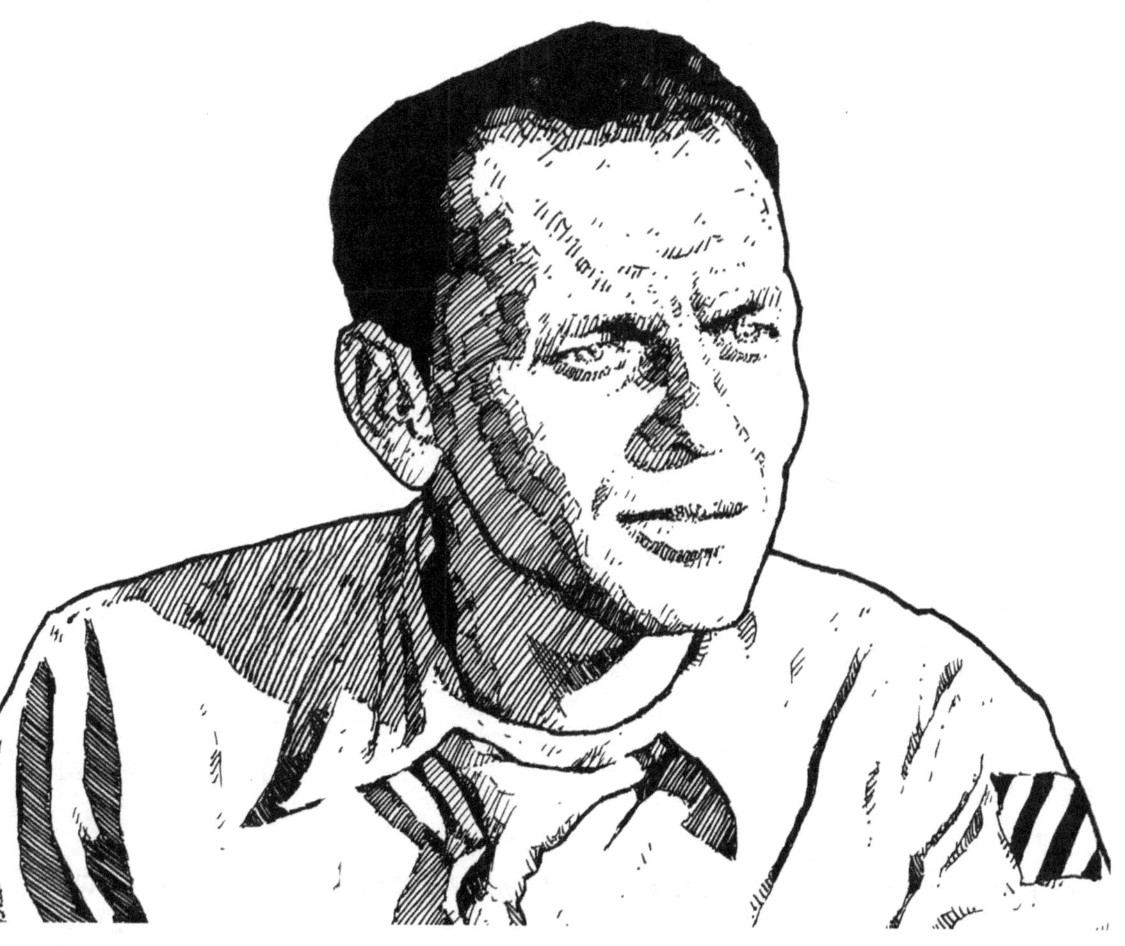

Dean Martin (born Dino Paul Crocetti) as Jeffrey Moss, **Bells Are Ringing** (1960)

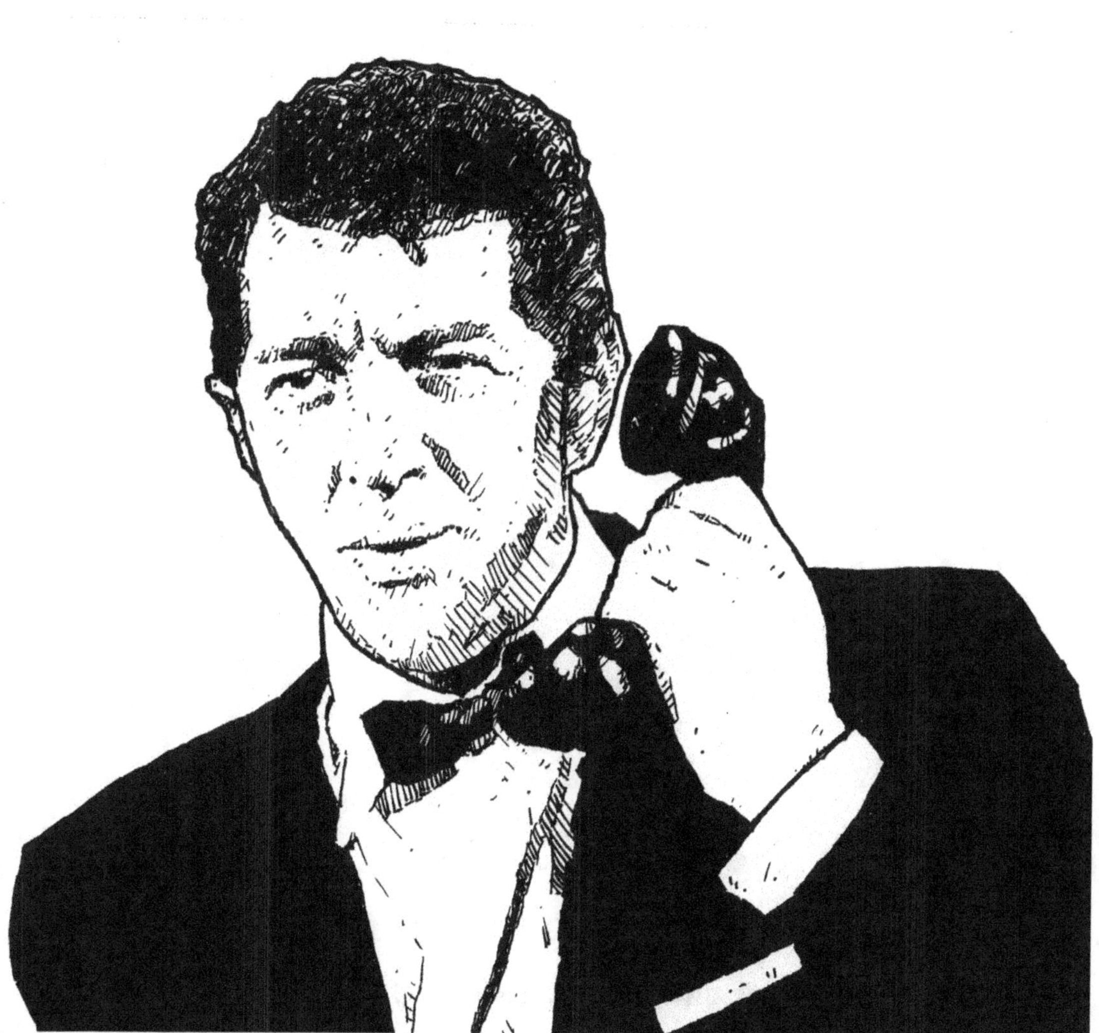

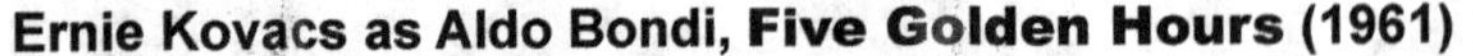

Ernie Kovacs as Aldo Bondi, Five Golden Hours (1961)

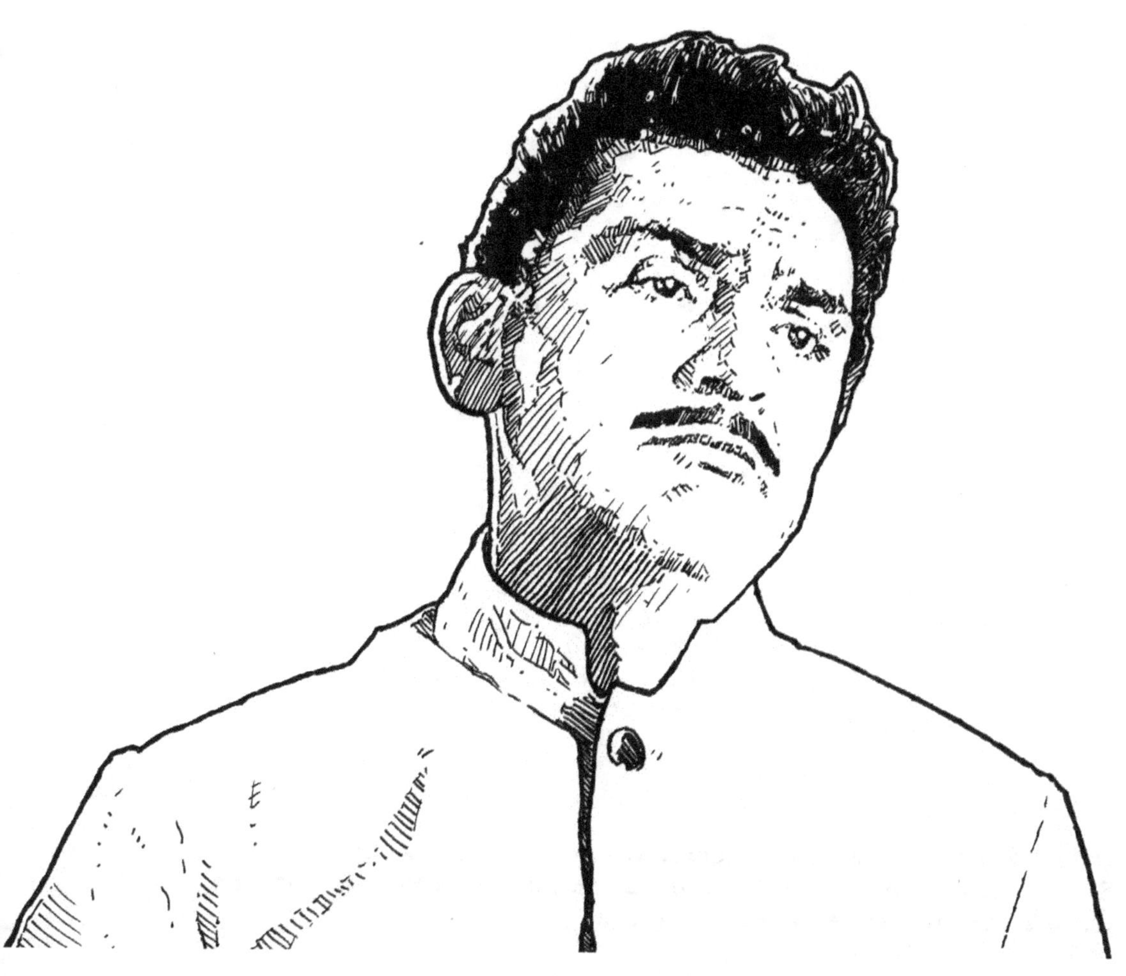

Natalie Wood (born Natalia Nikolaevna Zakharenko) as Angie Rossini,
Steve McQueen (born Terrence Stephen McQueen) as Rocky Papasano,
Love With the Proper Stranger (1963)

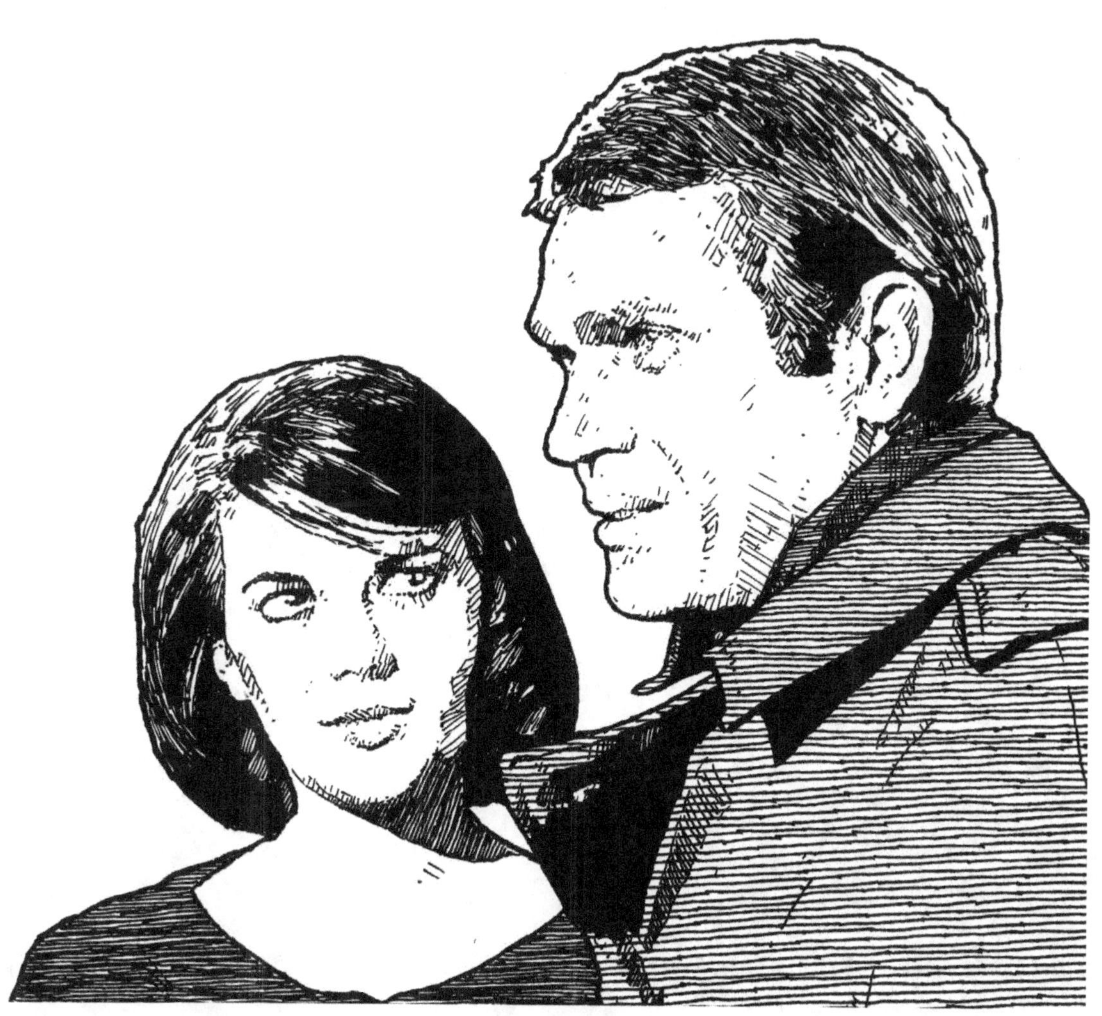

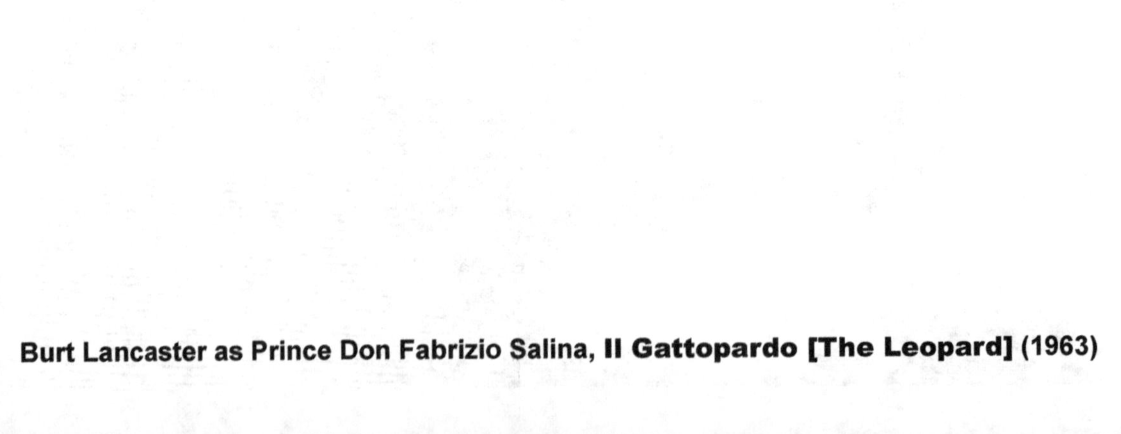

Burt Lancaster as Prince Don Fabrizio Salina, Il Gattopardo [The Leopard] (1963)

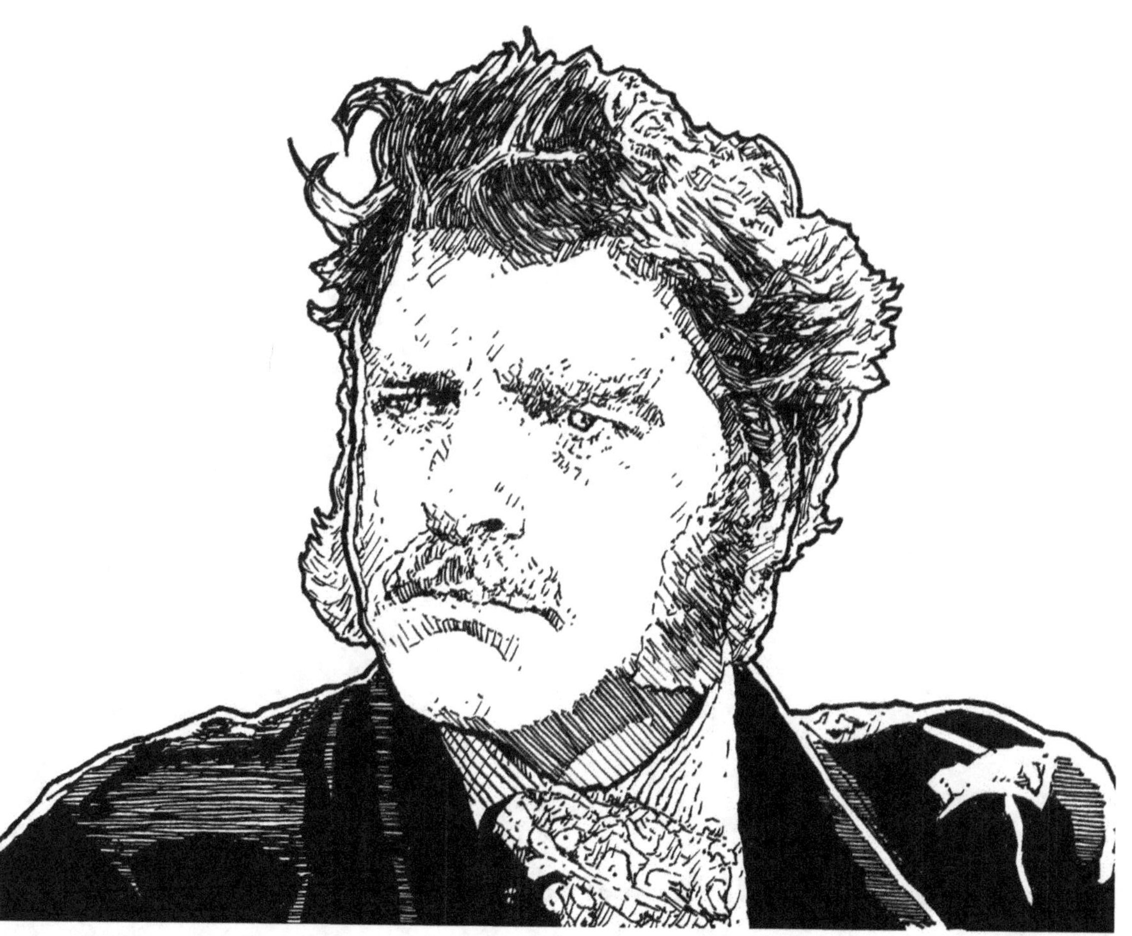

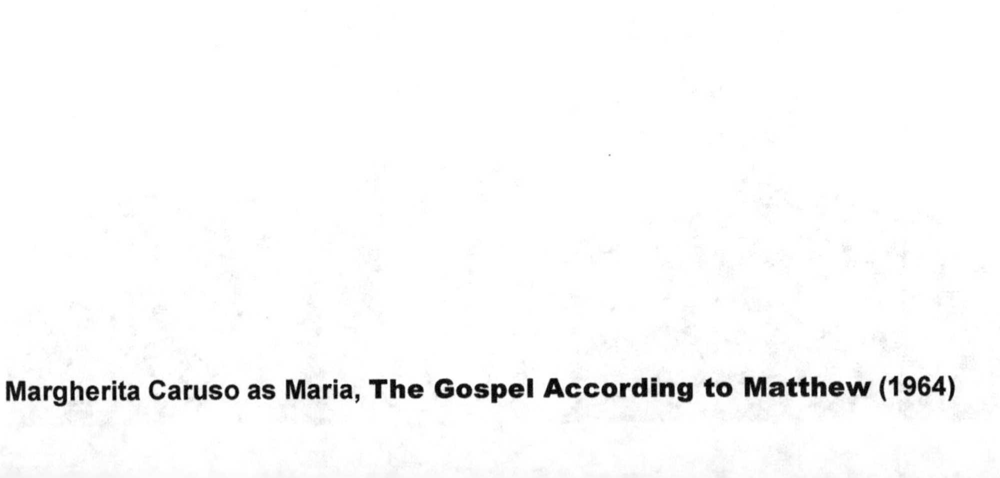

Margherita Caruso as Maria, **The Gospel According to Matthew** (1964)

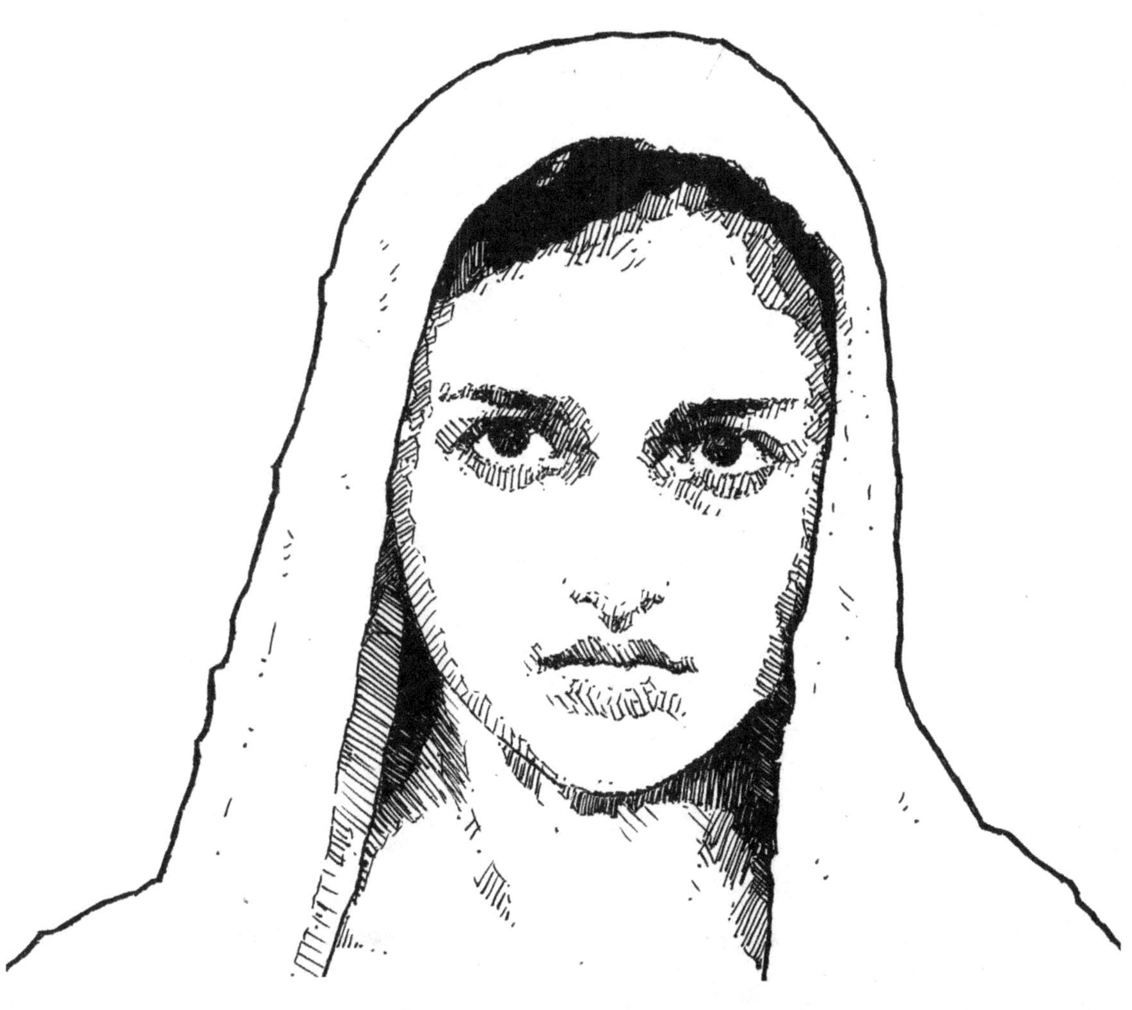

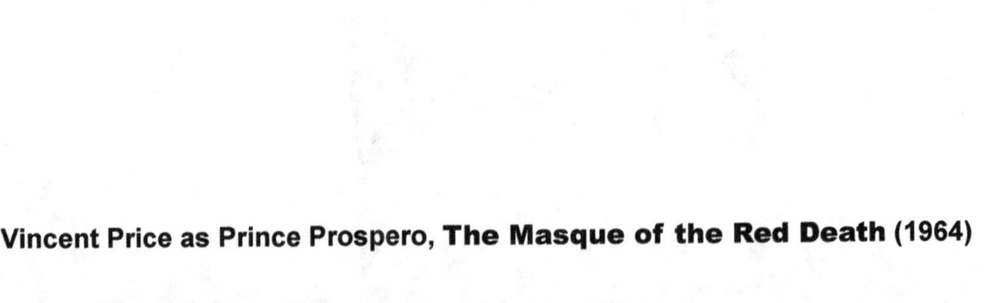

Vincent Price as Prince Prospero, The Masque of the Red Death (1964)

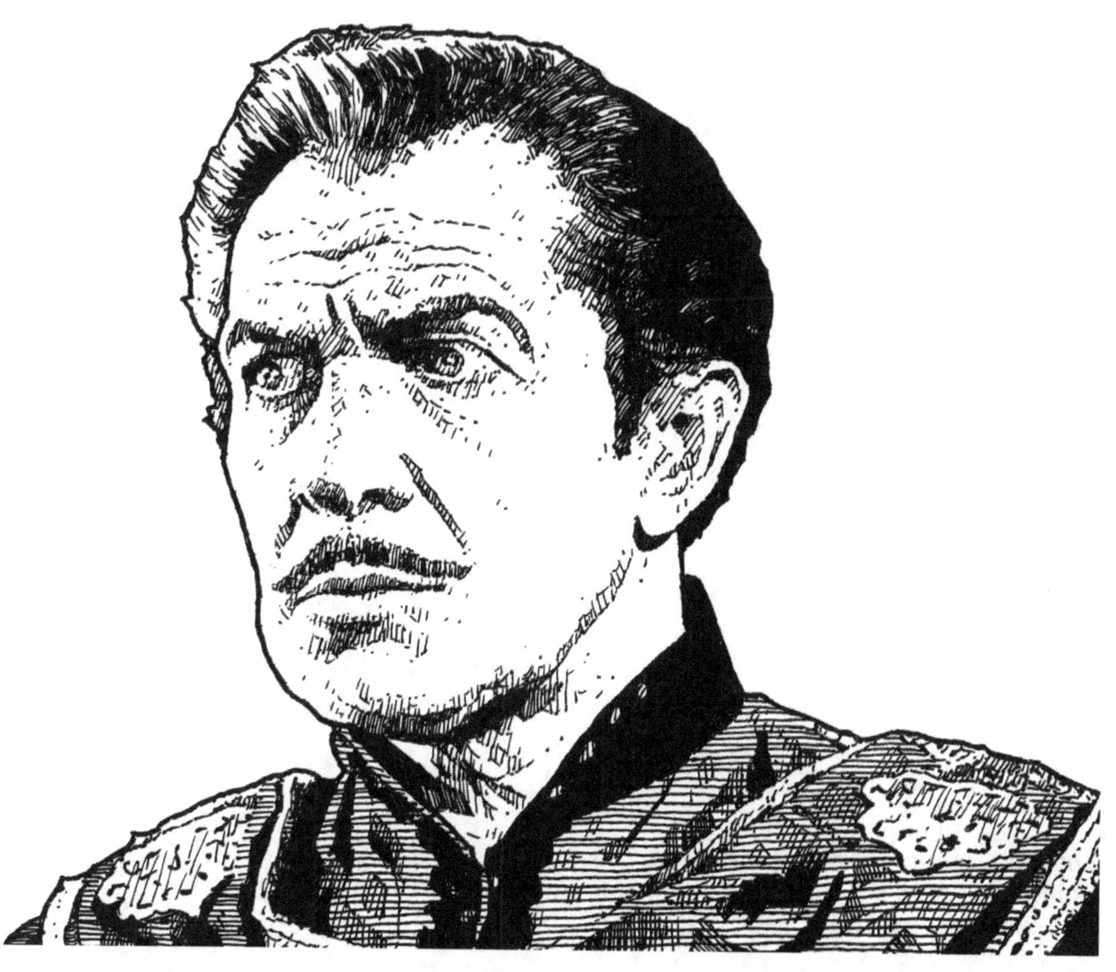

Charlton Heston (born John Charles Carter)
as Michelangelo di Lodovico Buonarroti Simoni,
The Agony and the Ecstasy (1965)

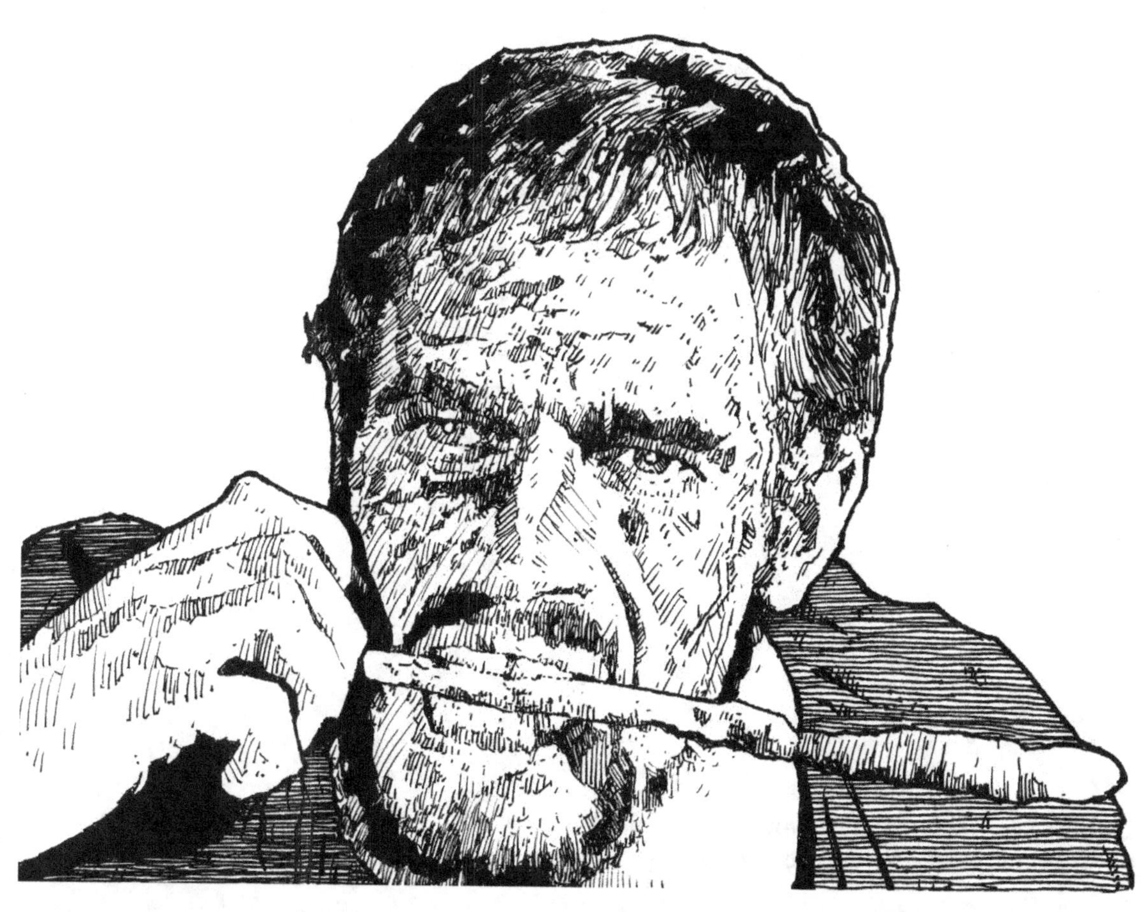

Liberace (born Władziu Valentino Liberace)
as Counsel Starker, **The Loved One** (1965)

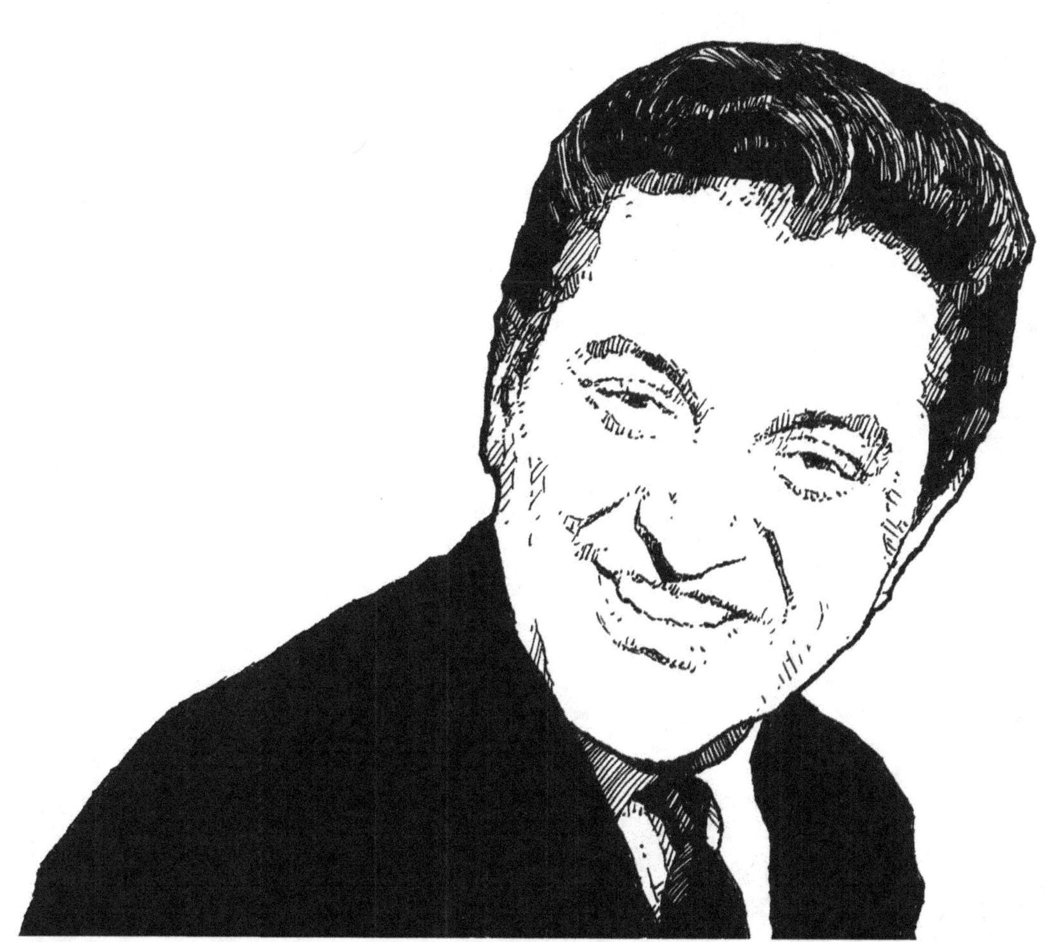

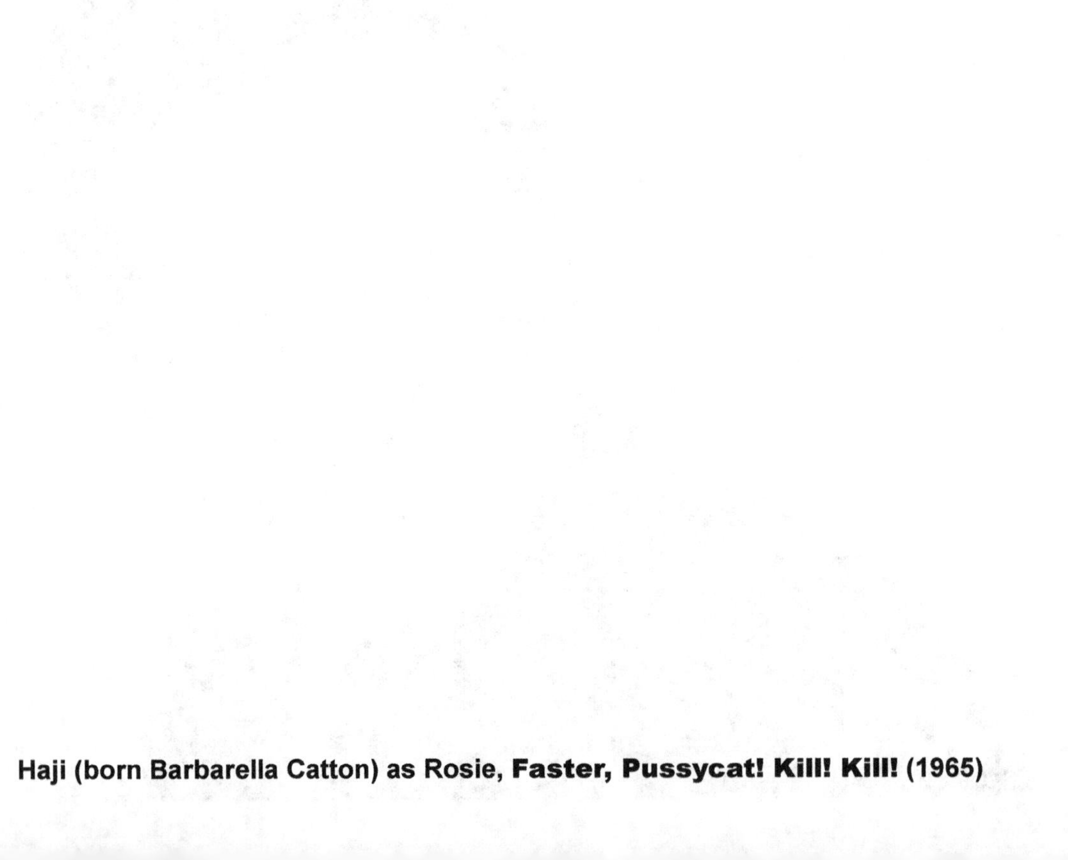

Haji (born Barbarella Catton) as Rosie, **Faster, Pussycat! Kill! Kill!** (1965)

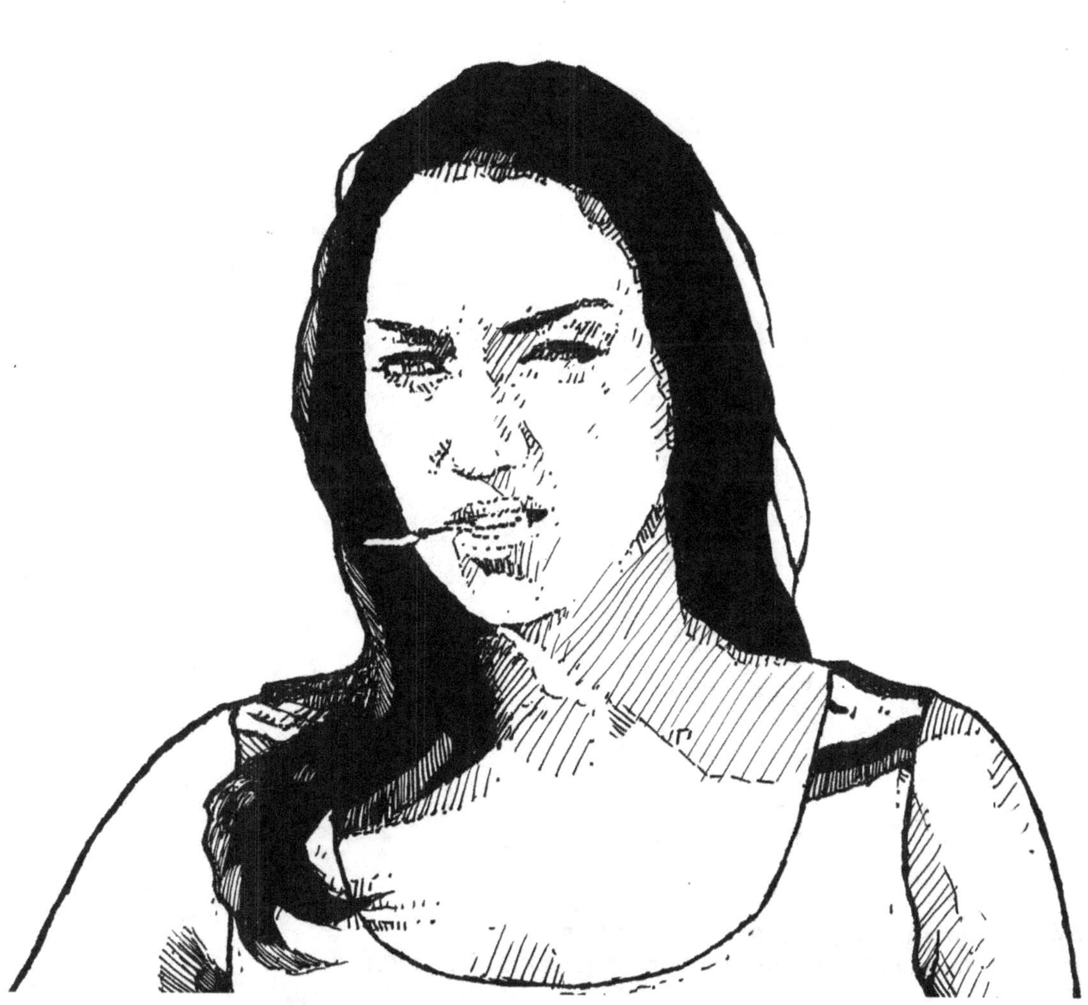

**Peter Sellers (born Richard Henry Sellers)
as Aldo Vanucci (as Federico Fabrizi), After the Fox (1966)**

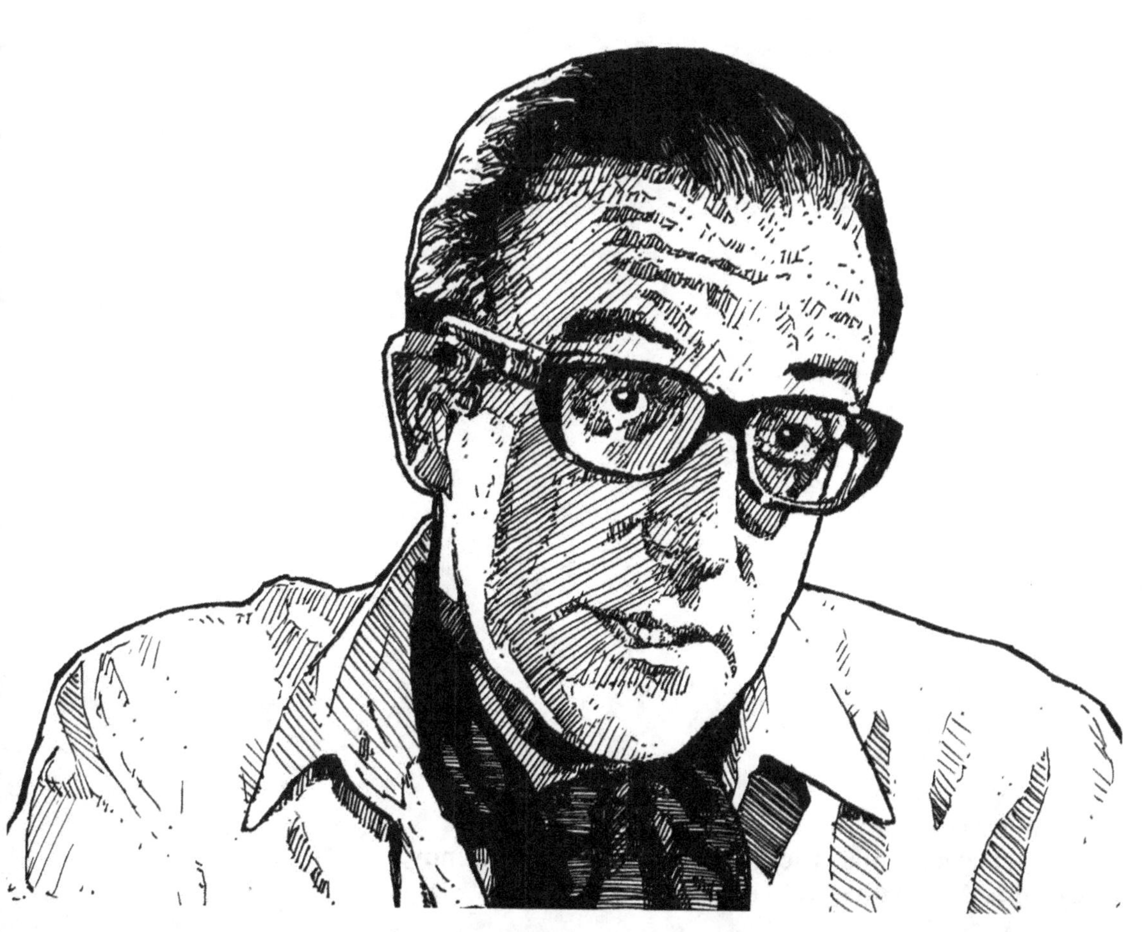

Marcello Mastroianni
as Grand Duke Nikolai "Nicky" Wladimirovitch Godunov,
Diamonds for Breakfast (1966)

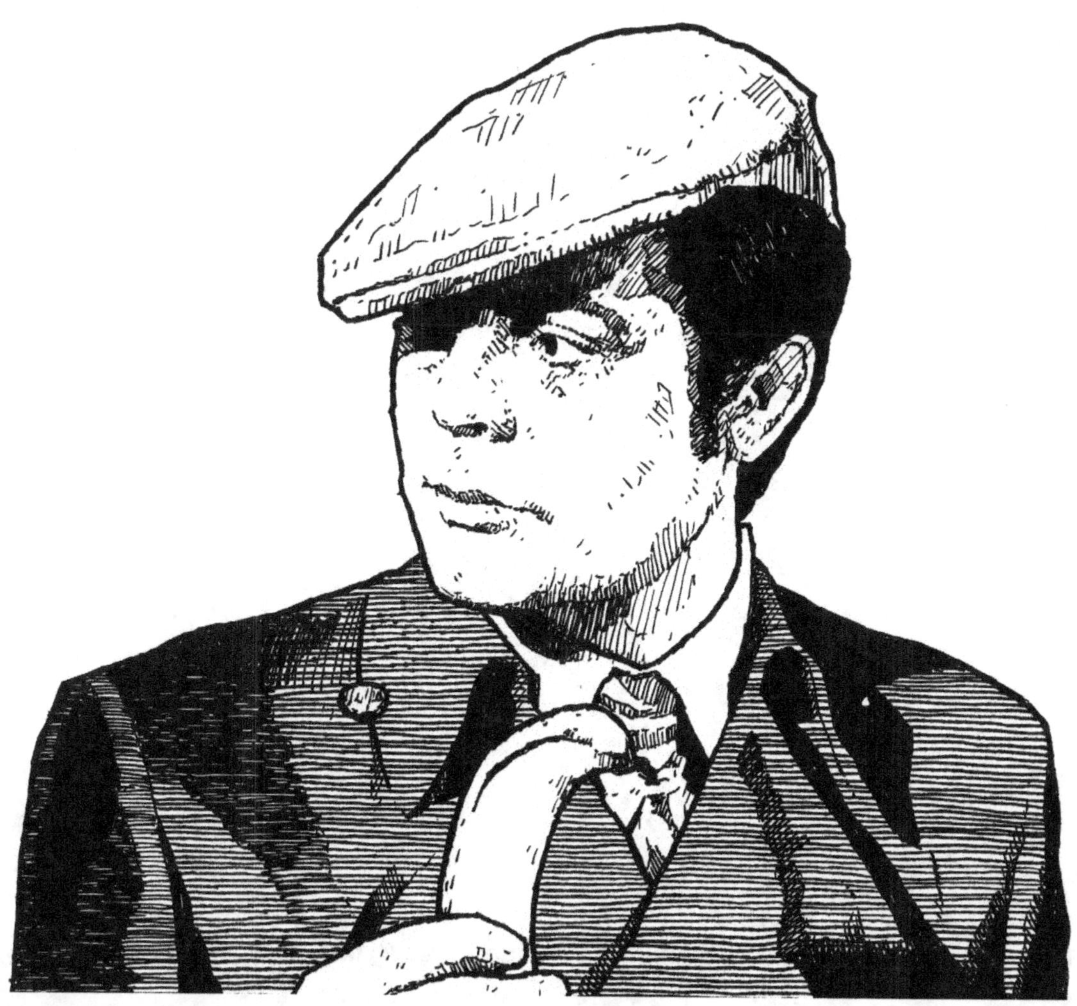

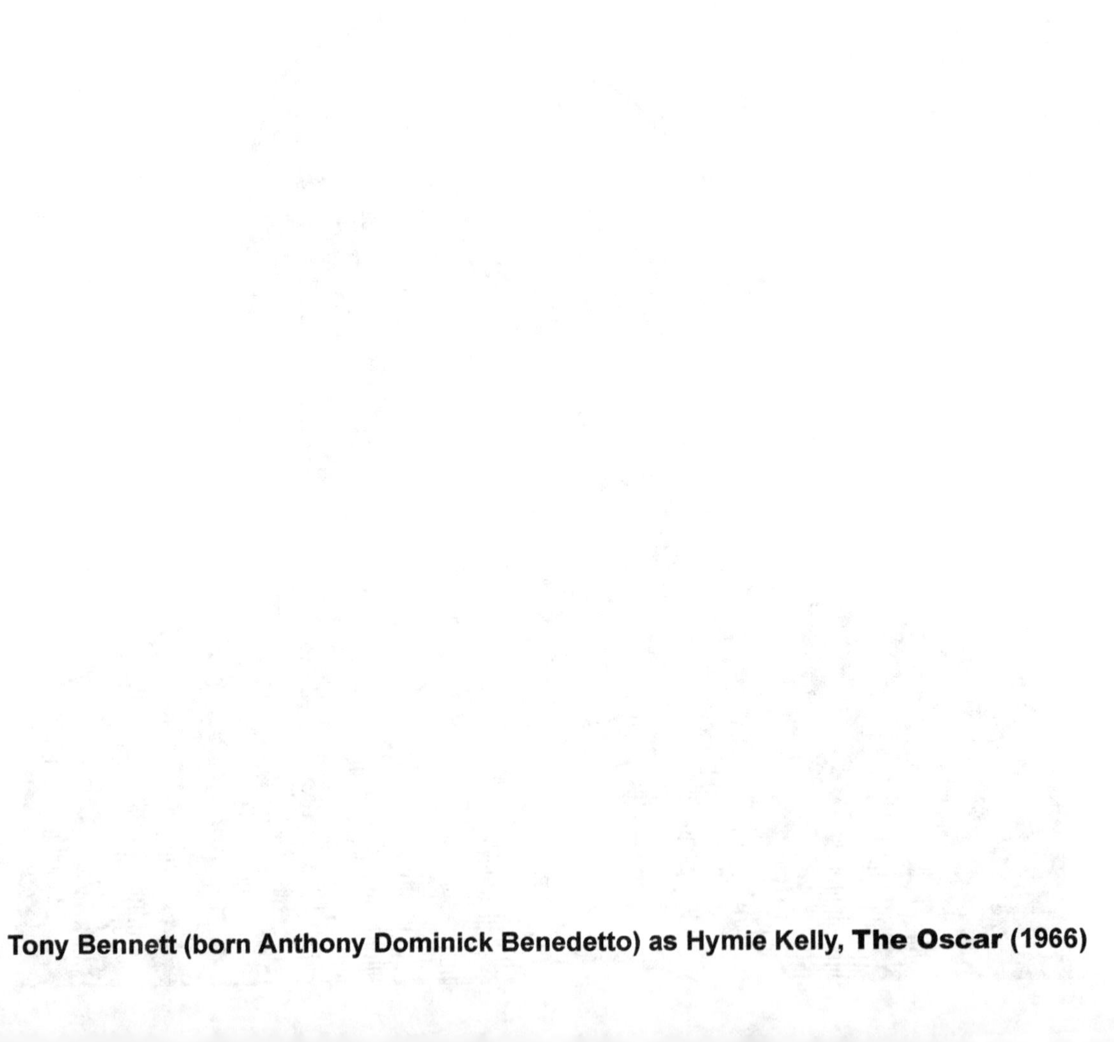

Tony Bennett (born Anthony Dominick Benedetto) as Hymie Kelly, **The Oscar** (1966)

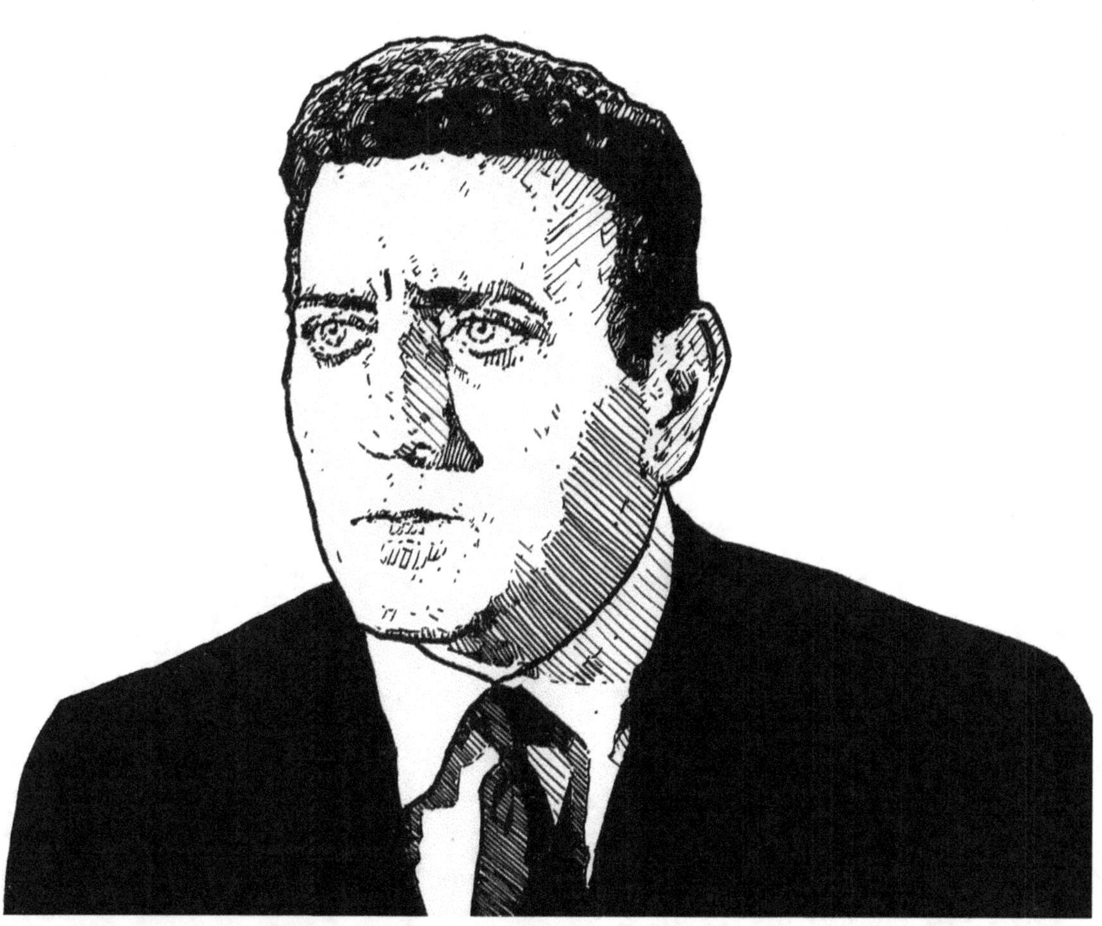

John Saxon (born Carmine Orrico) as Chuy Medena, **The Appaloosa** (1966)

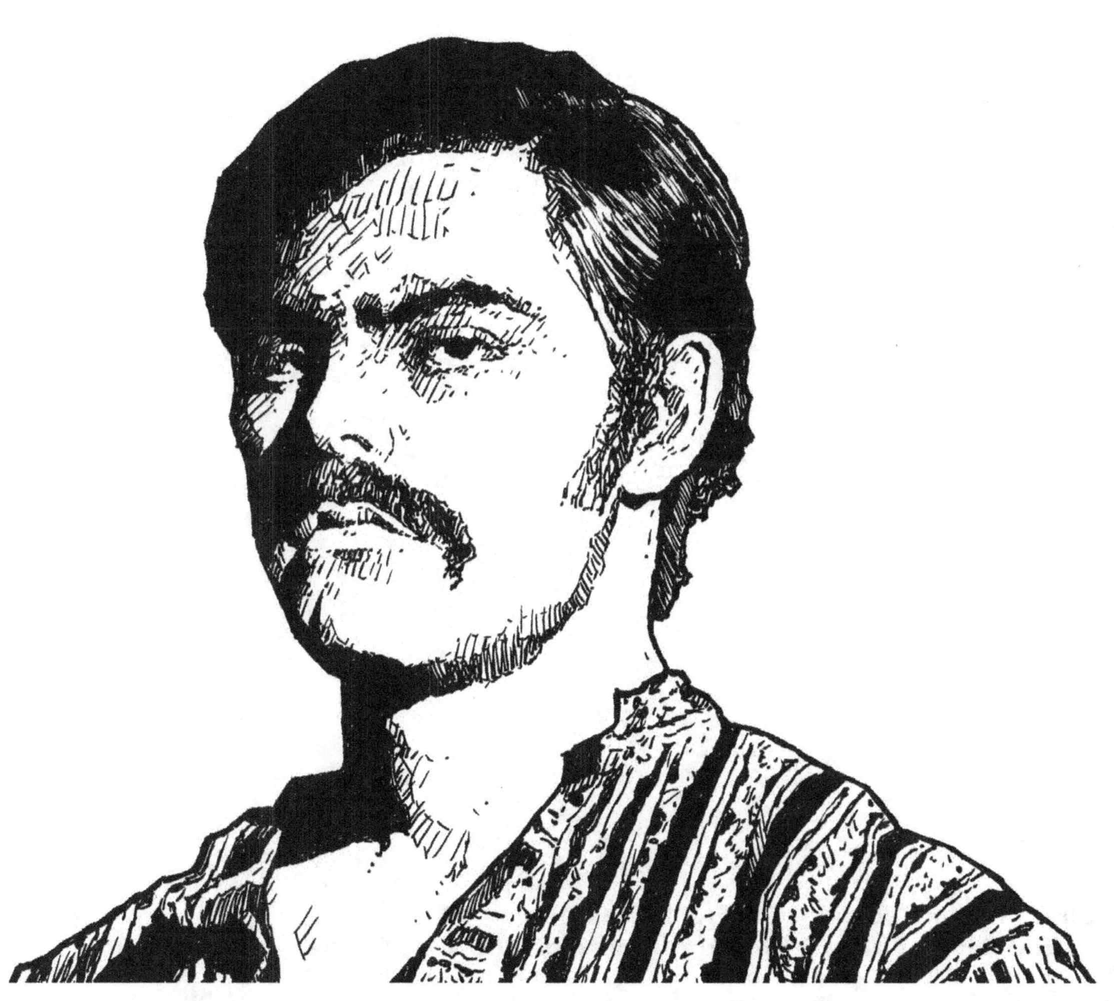

Buster Keaton (born Joseph Frank Keaton)
as Erronius, **A Funny Thing Happened on the Way to the Forum** (1966)

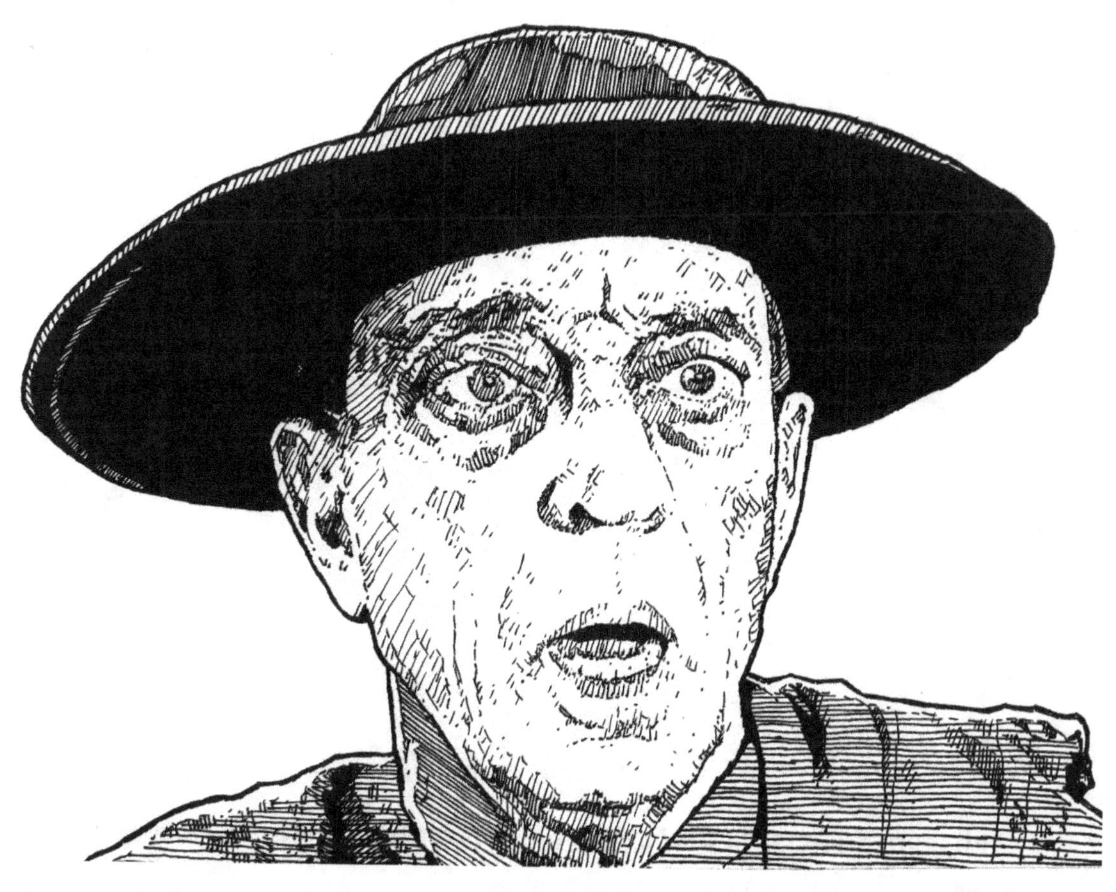

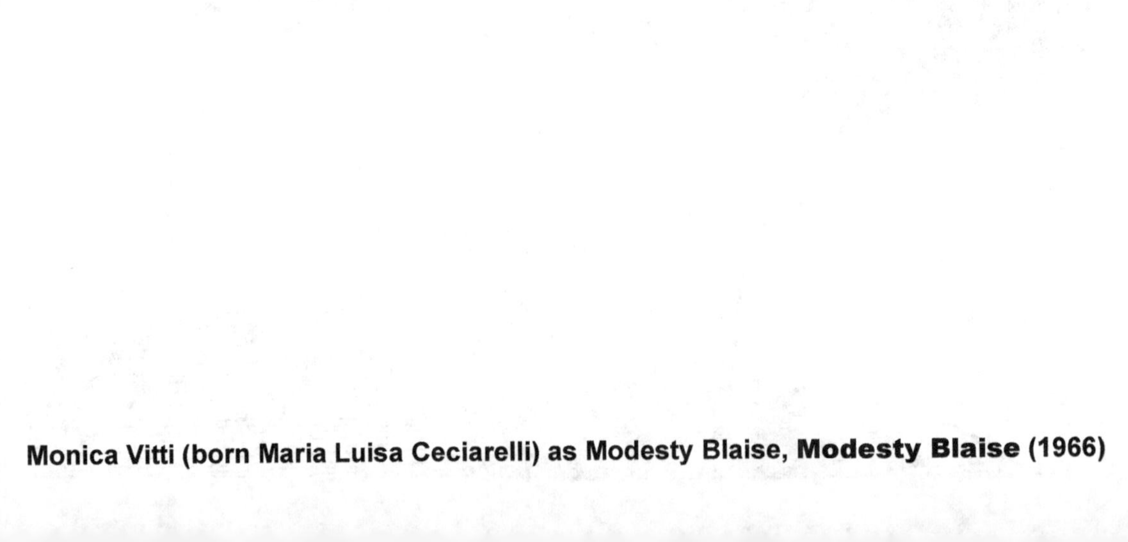

Monica Vitti (born Maria Luisa Ceciarelli) as Modesty Blaise, **Modesty Blaise** (1966)

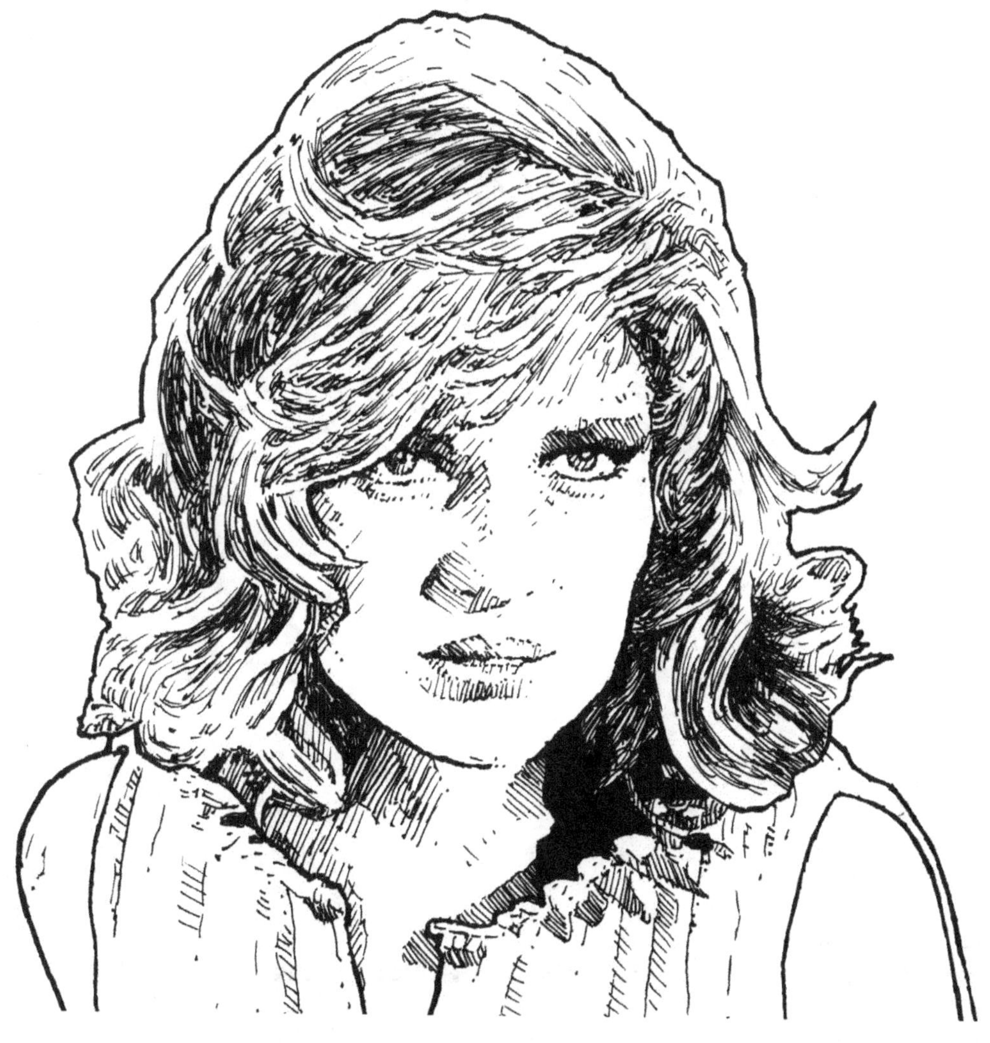

Gian Maria Volonté
as El Chuncho Munoz, **Quién sabe? [A Bullet for the General]** (1966)

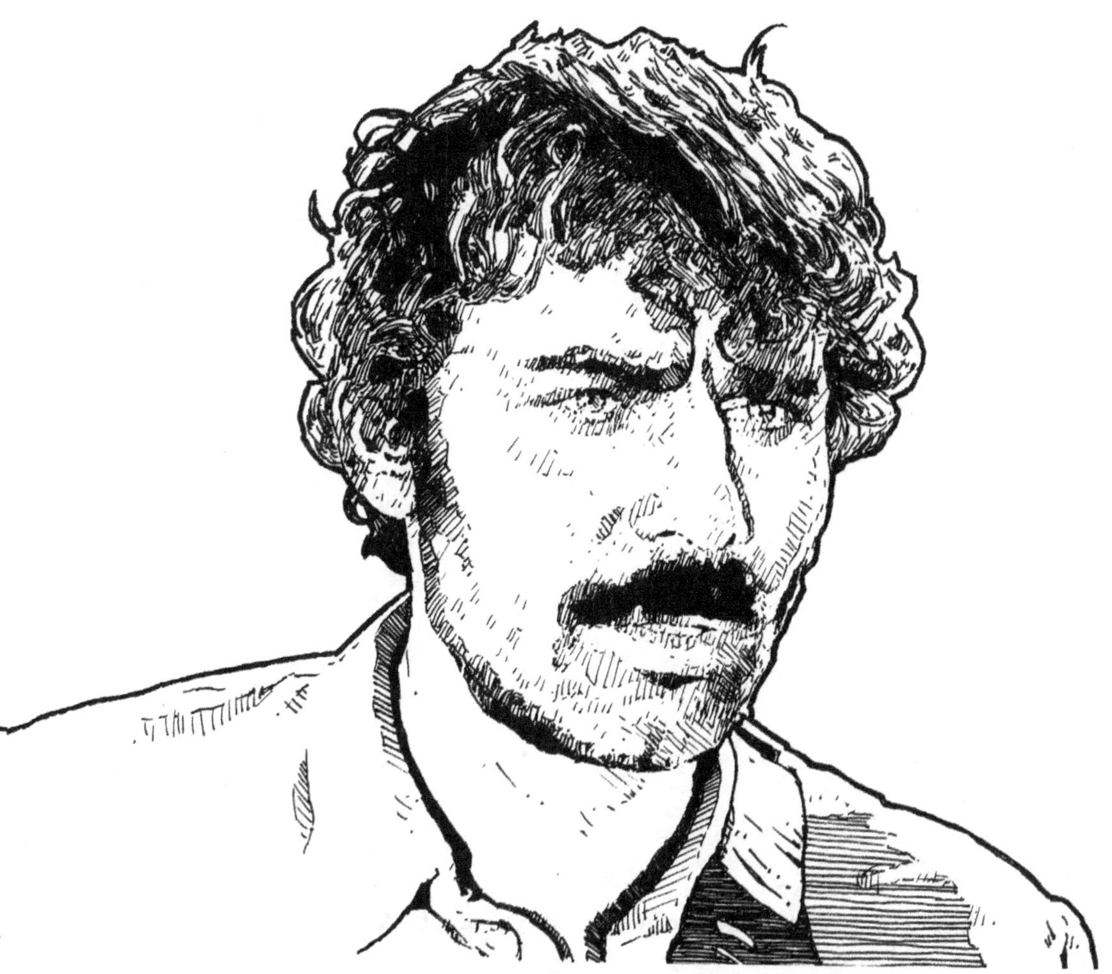

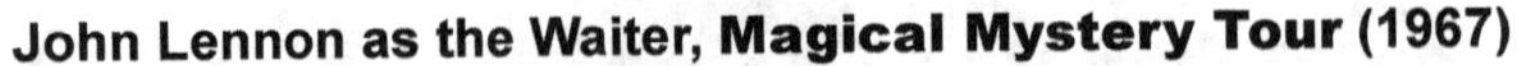

John Lennon as the Waiter, Magical Mystery Tour (1967)

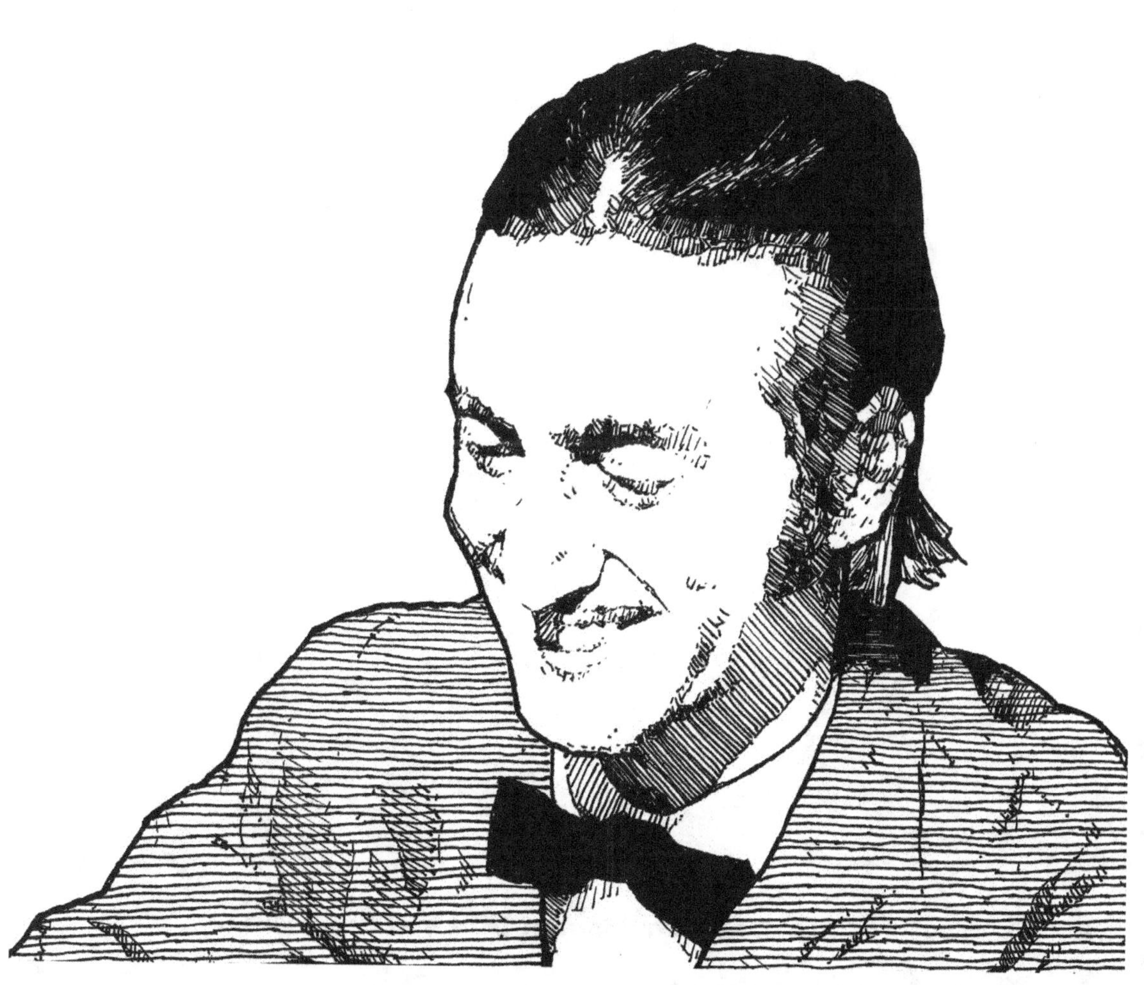

Pier Paolo Pasolini as Don Juan, **Requiescant [Kill and Pray]** (1967)

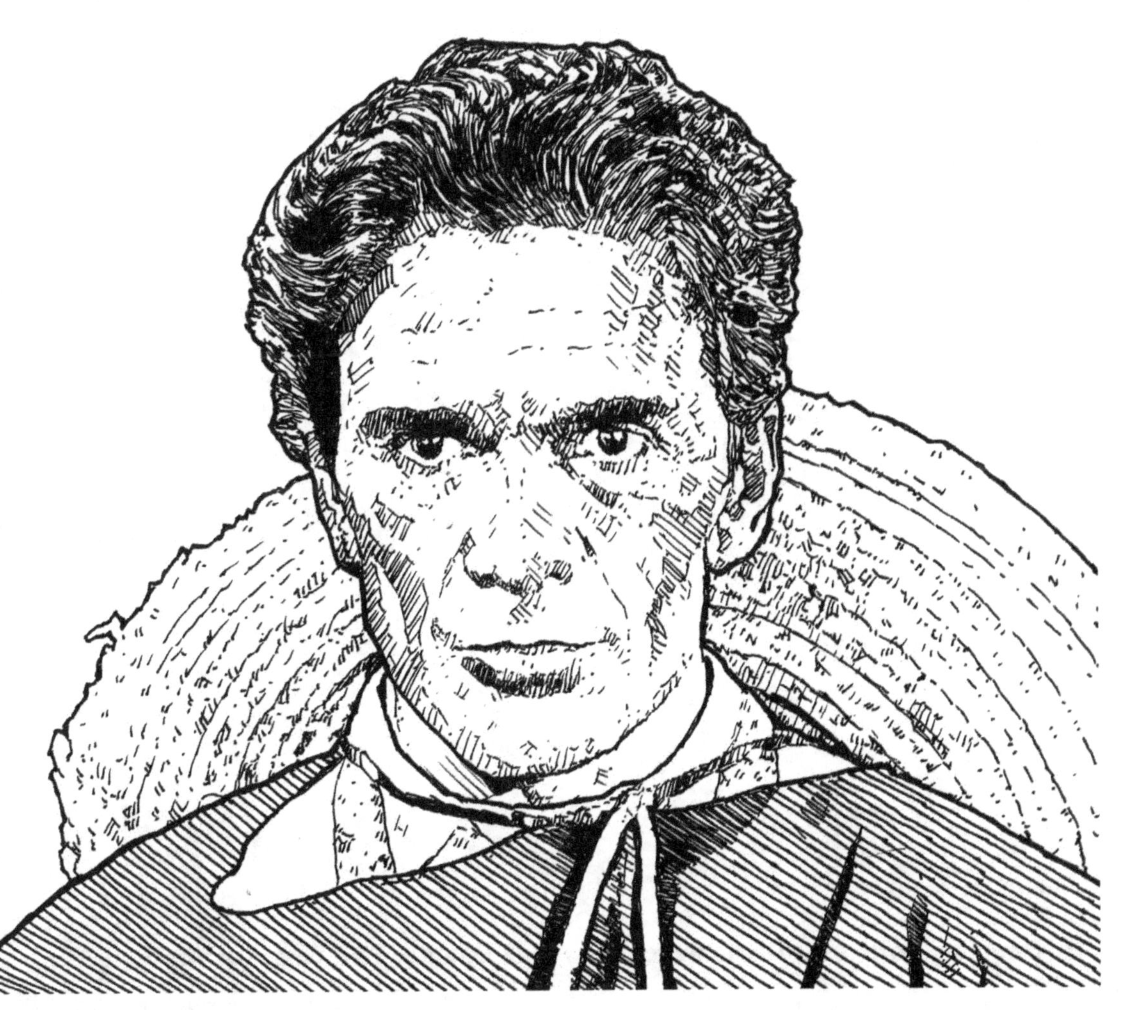

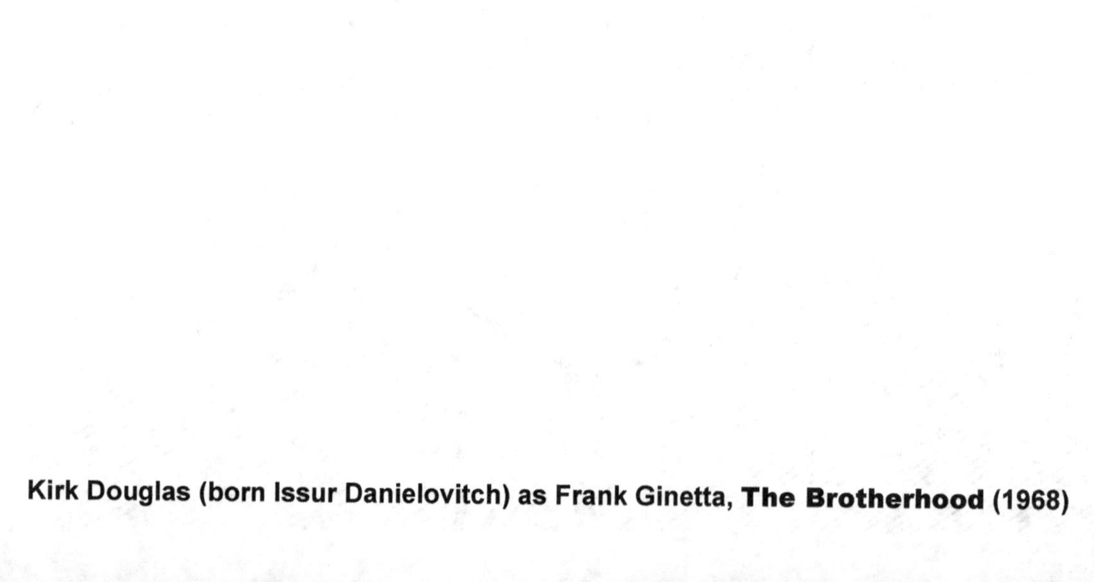

Kirk Douglas (born Issur Danielovitch) as Frank Ginetta, **The Brotherhood** (1968)

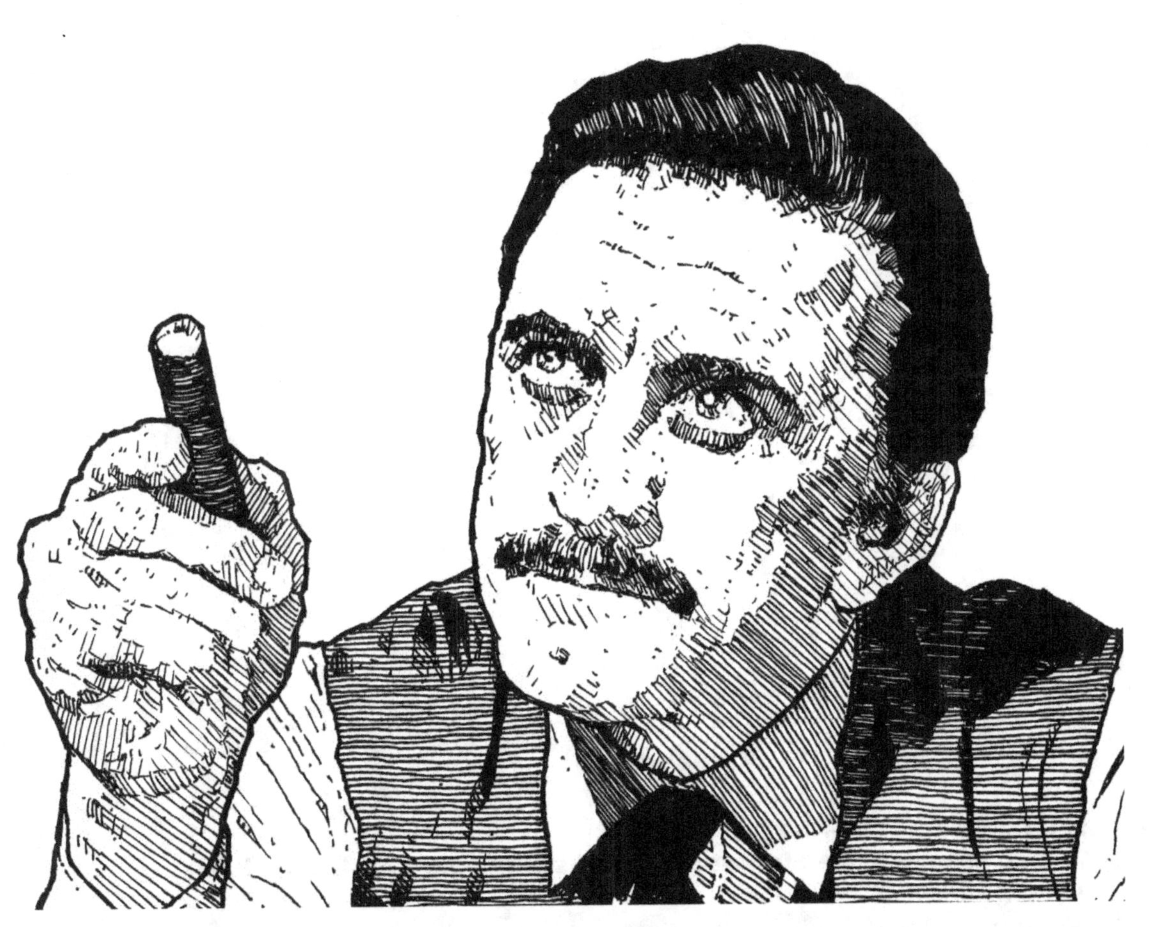

Jean Gabin (born Jean-Alexis Moncorgé)
as Vittorio Manalese, **Le clan des Siciliens [The Sicilian Clan]** (1969)

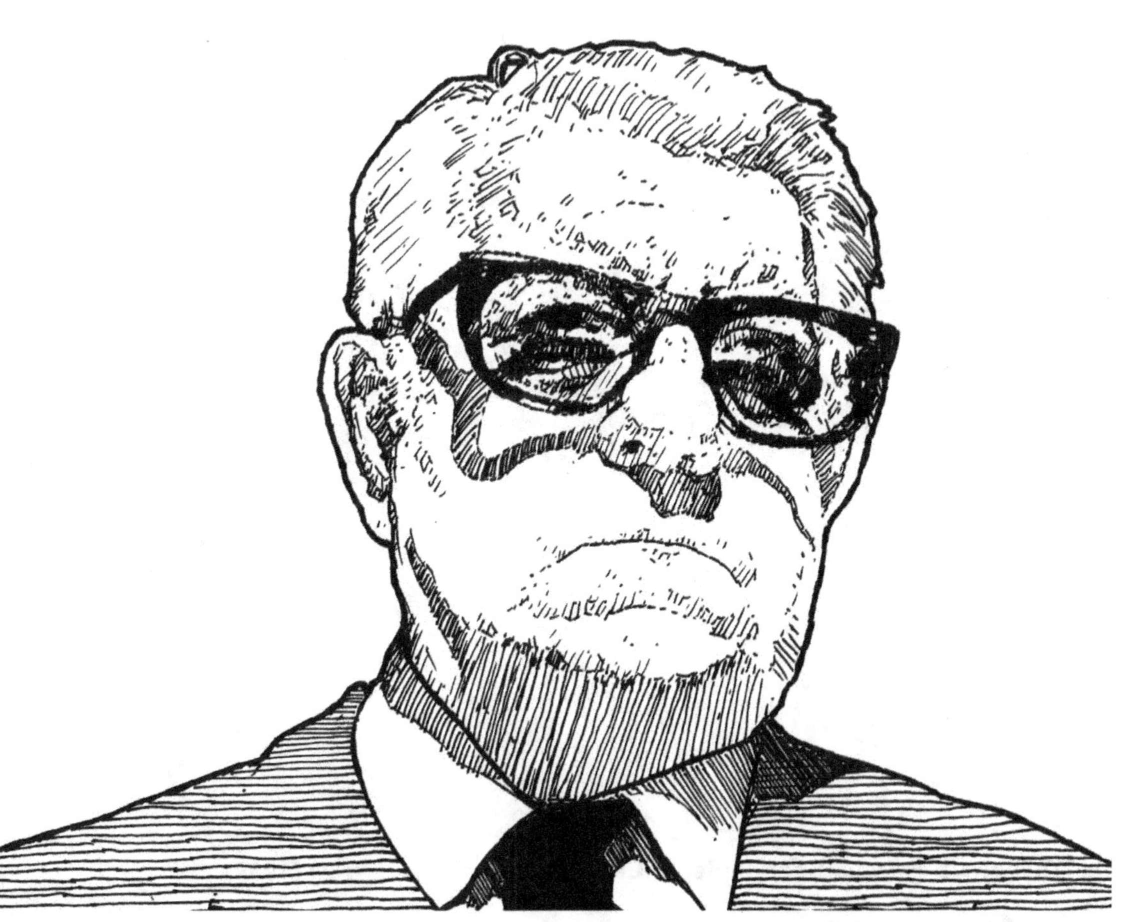

Eli Wallach as Frankie Scannapieco, **Le cerveau [The Brain]** (1969)

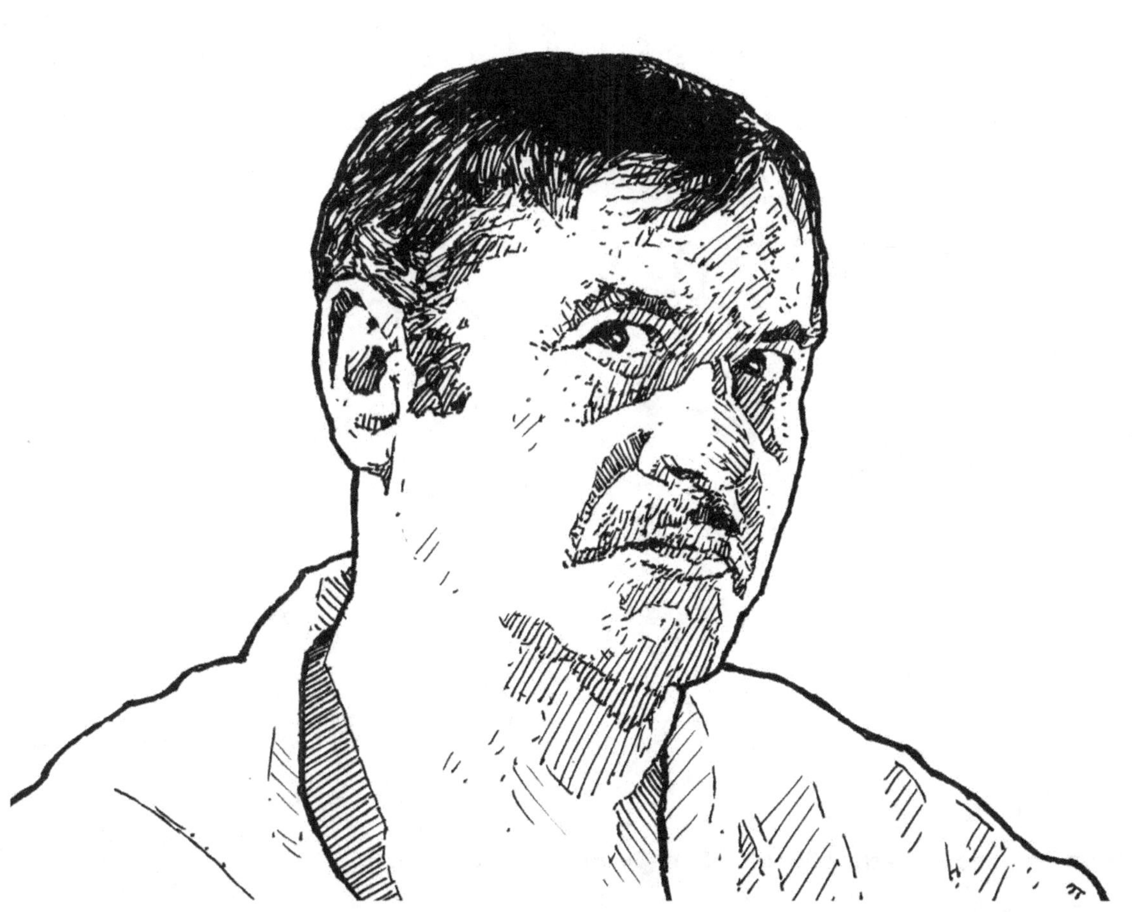

Dom DeLuise as Father Fyodor, The Twelve Chairs (1970)

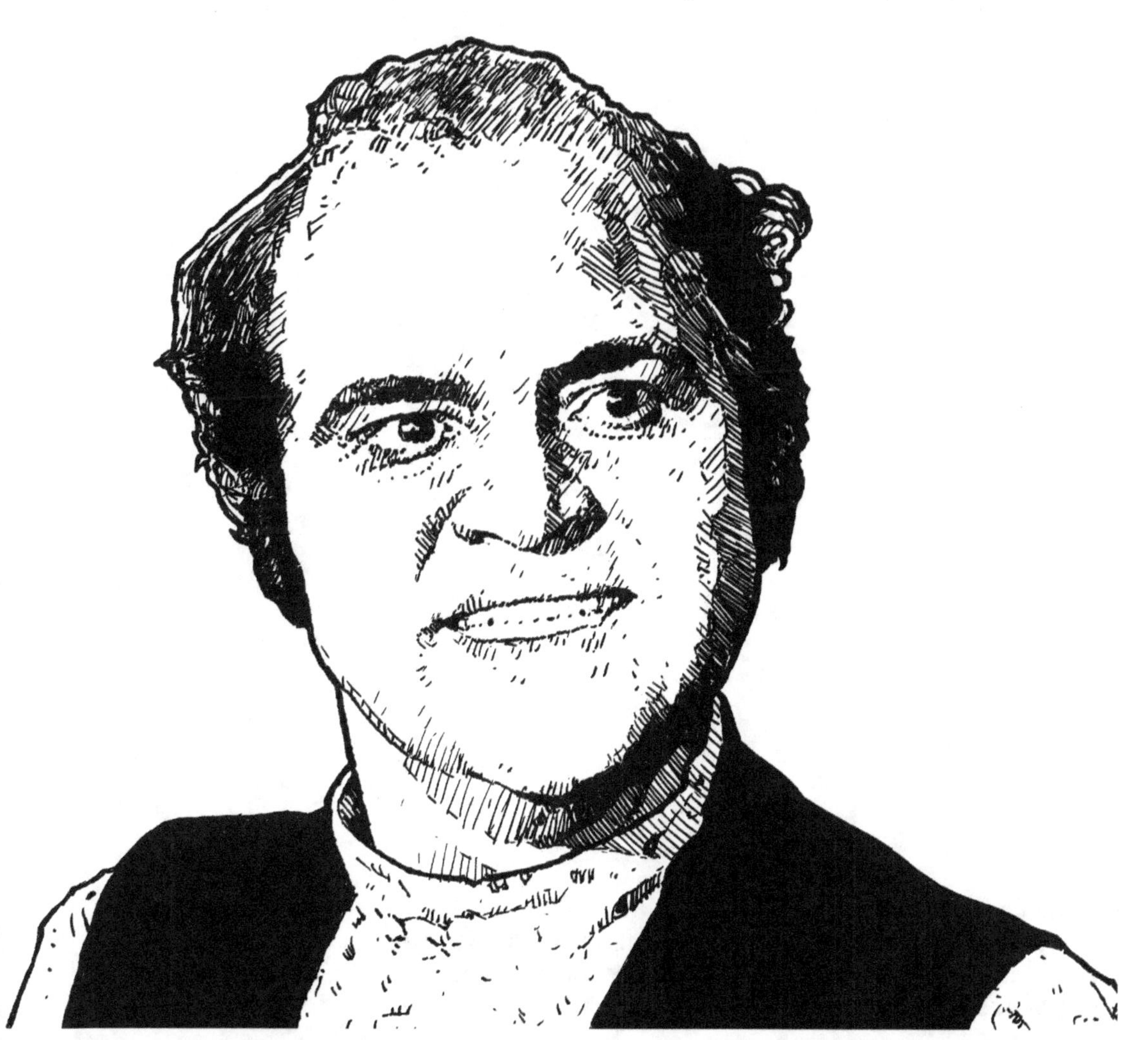

Lousie Lasser as Gina,
Woody Allen (born Allan Stewart Konigsberg) as Fabrizio,
Everything You Always Wanted to Know About Sex*
***But Were Afraid to Ask (1972)**

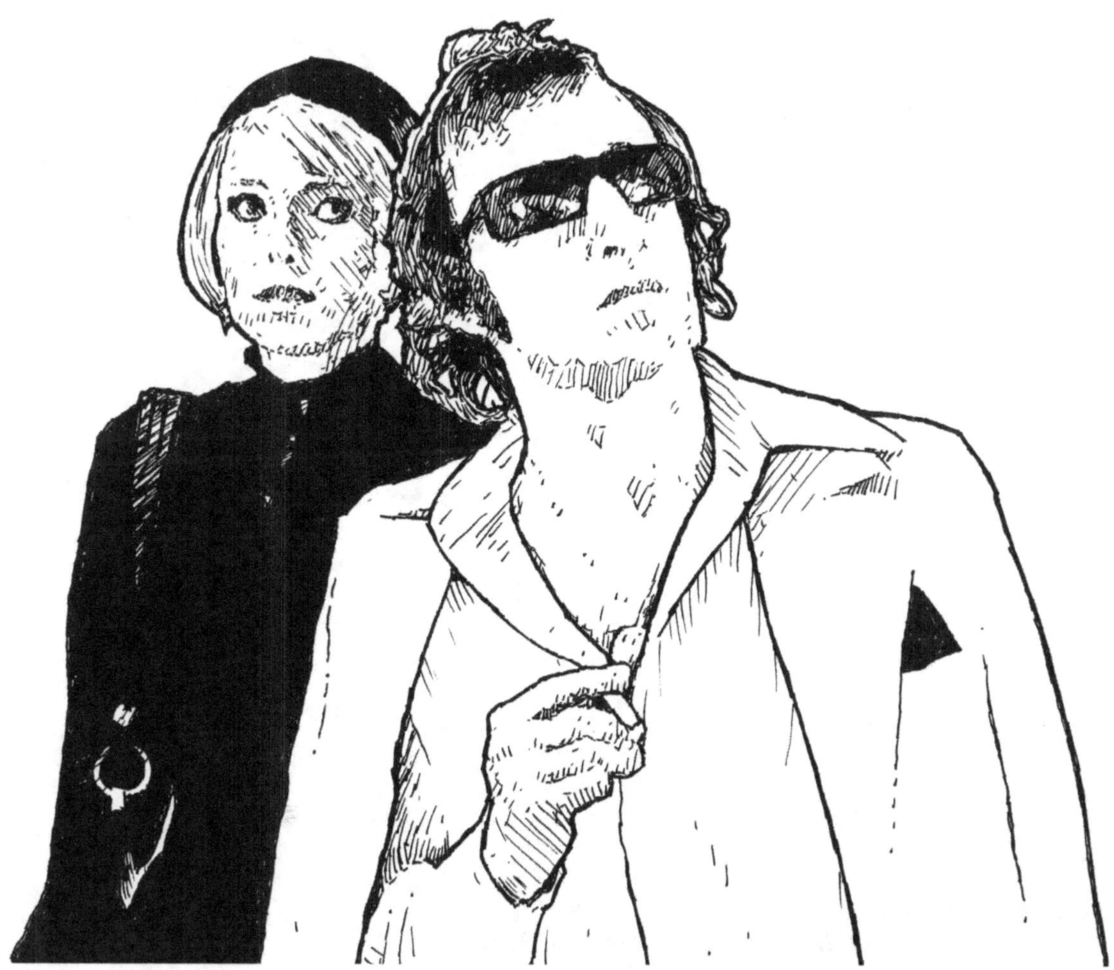

**Sophia Loren (born Sofia Villani Scicolone)
as Aldonza/Dulcinea, Man of La Mancha (1972)**

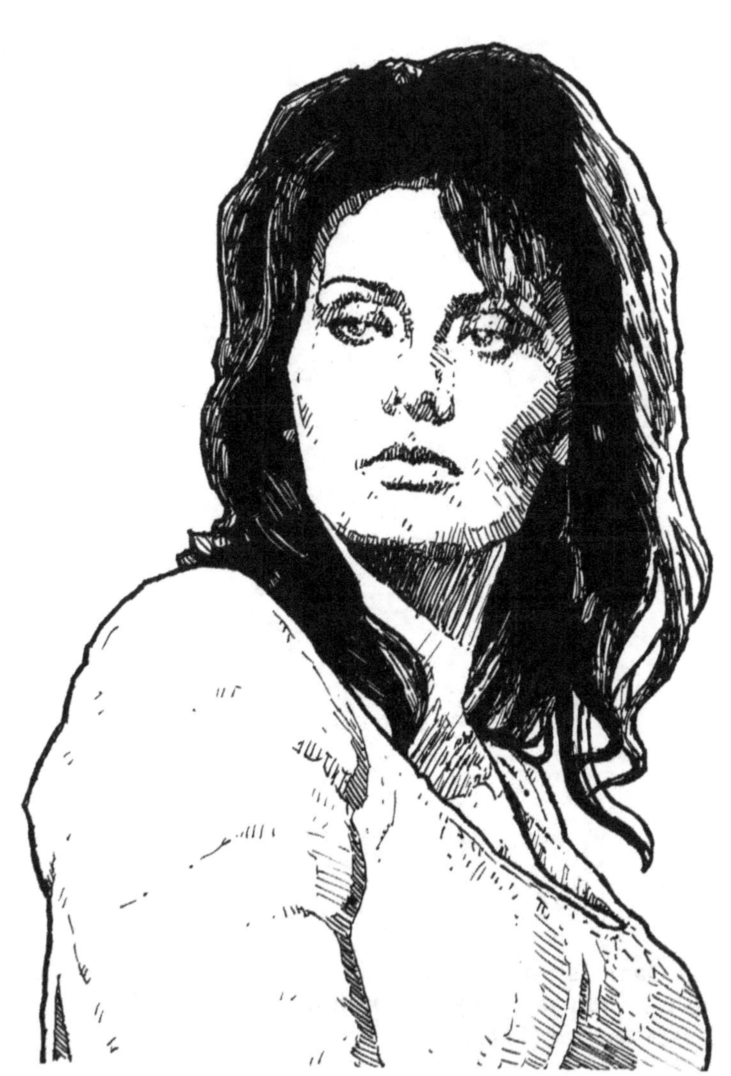

James Caan as Sonny Corleone,
Marlon Brando as Don Vito Corleone,
The Godfather (1972)

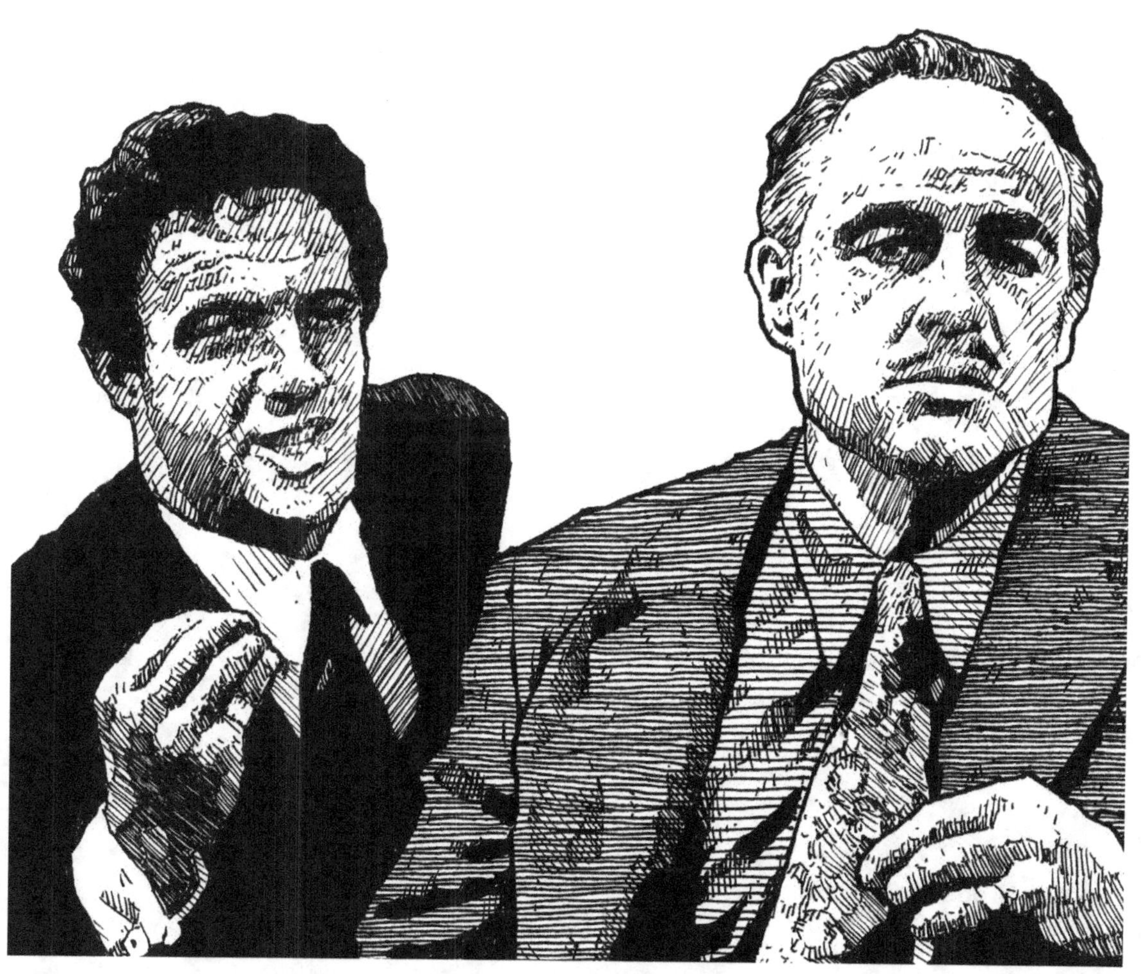

Charles Bronson (born Charles Dennis Buchinsky) as Joe Valachi, **The Valachi Papers** (1972)

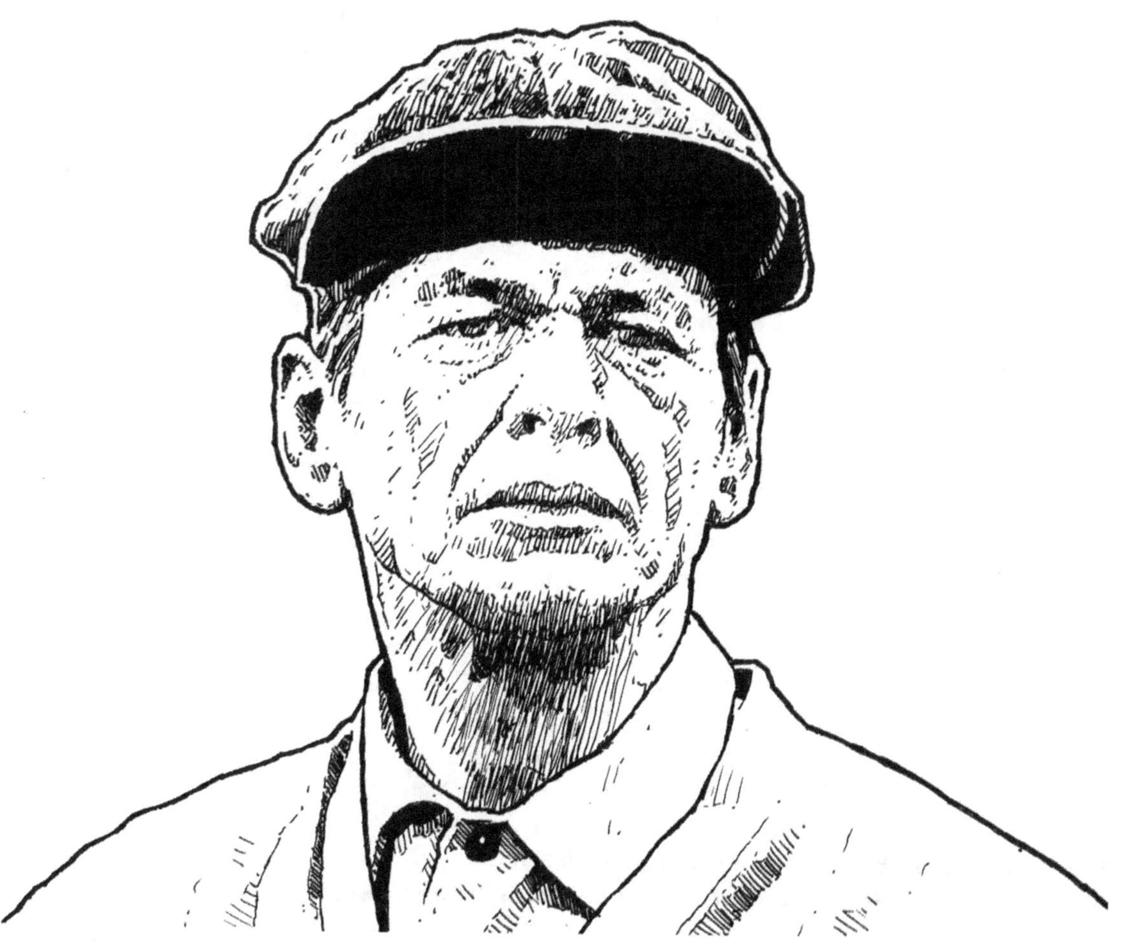

Florinda Bolkan (born Florinda Soares Bulcão)
as Clara Mataro, **Una breve vacanza [A Brief Vacation]** (1973)

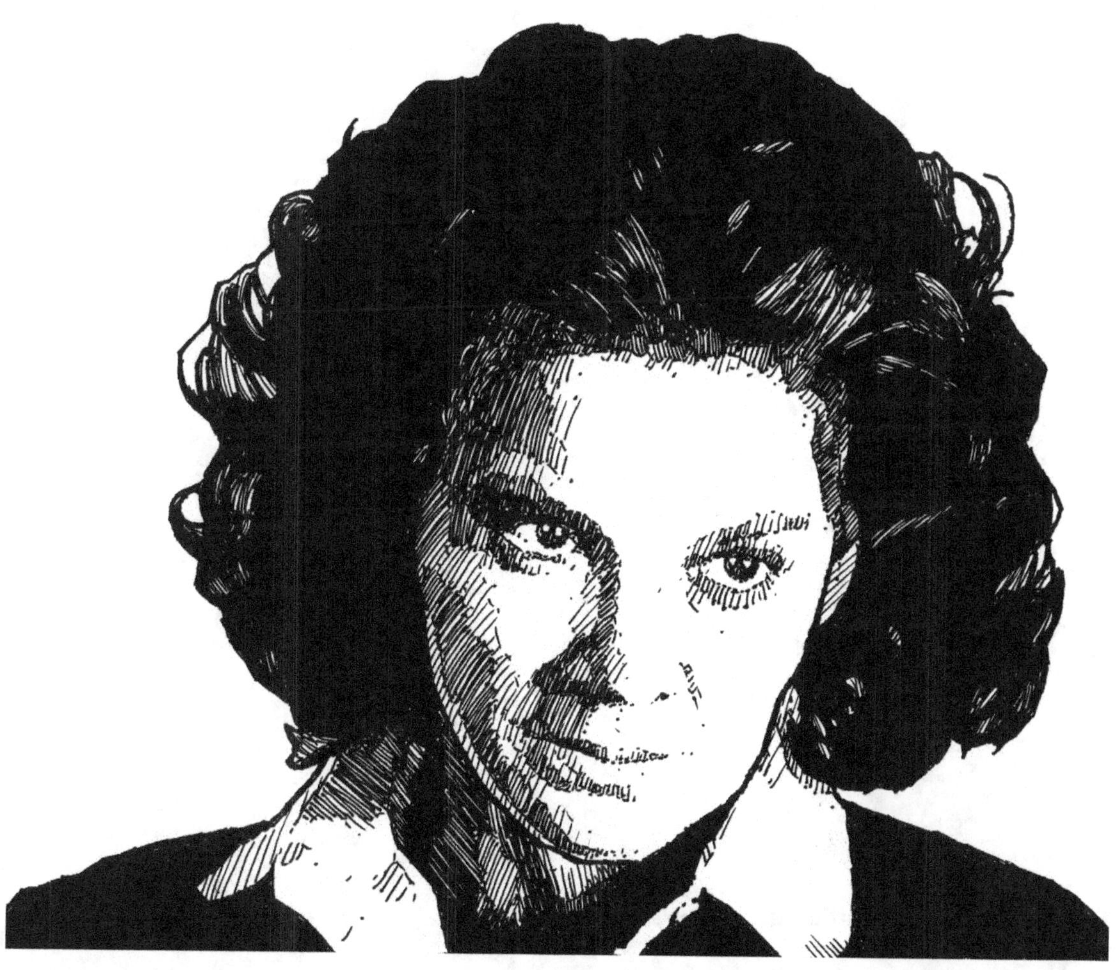

Harvey Keitel as Charlie, Mean Streets (1973)

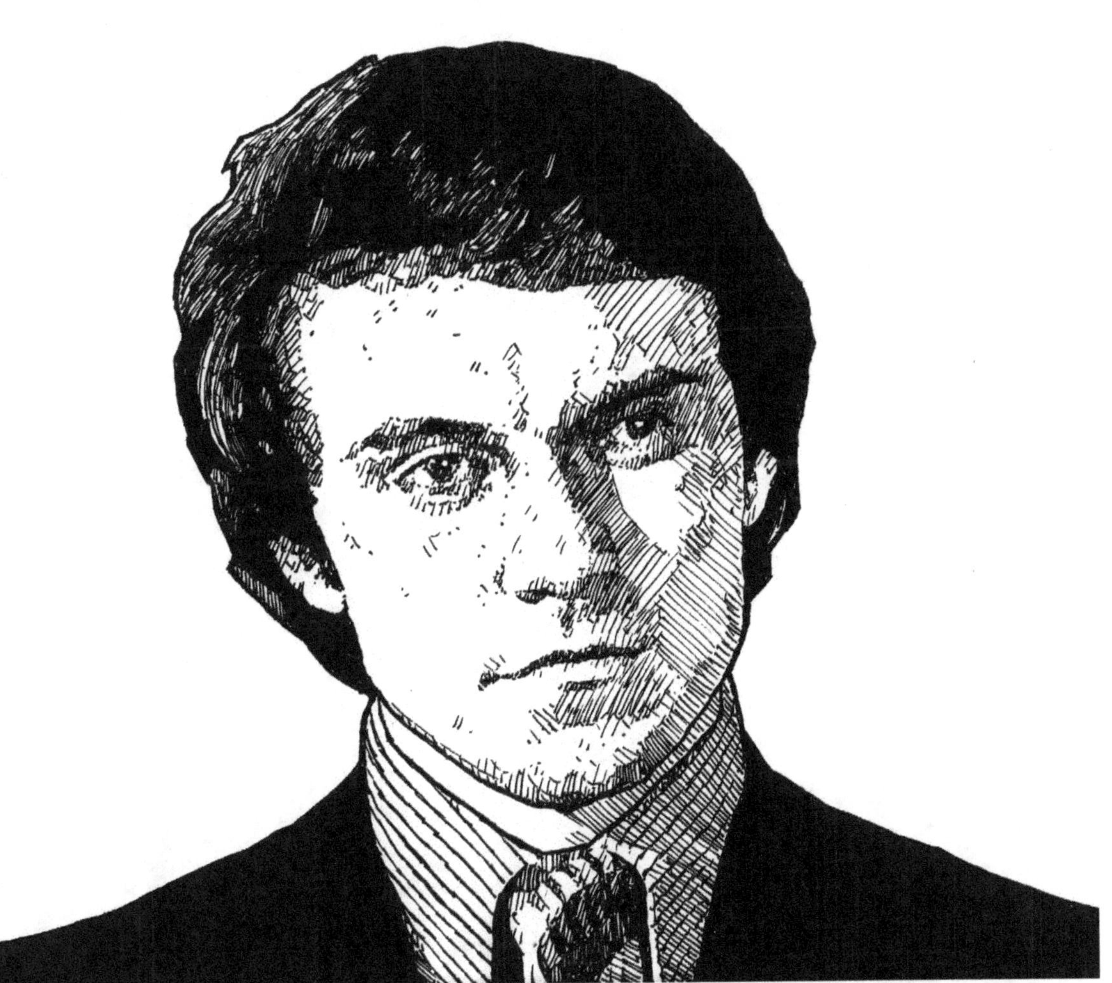

Oliver Reed (born Robert Oliver Reed) as Vito Cipriani, **Revolver** (1973)

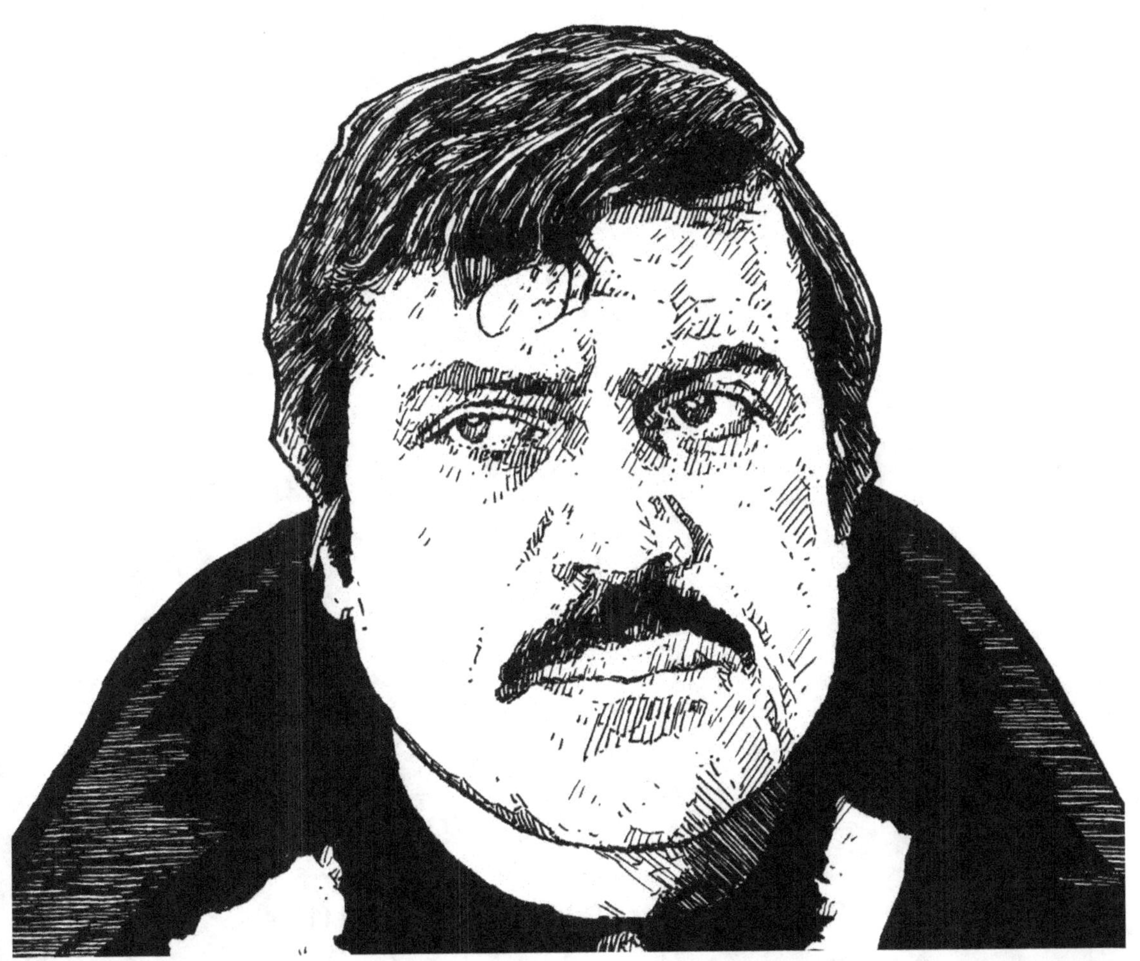

Joan Collins as Elena Sperani, **L'arbitro** [**Playing the Field**] (1974)

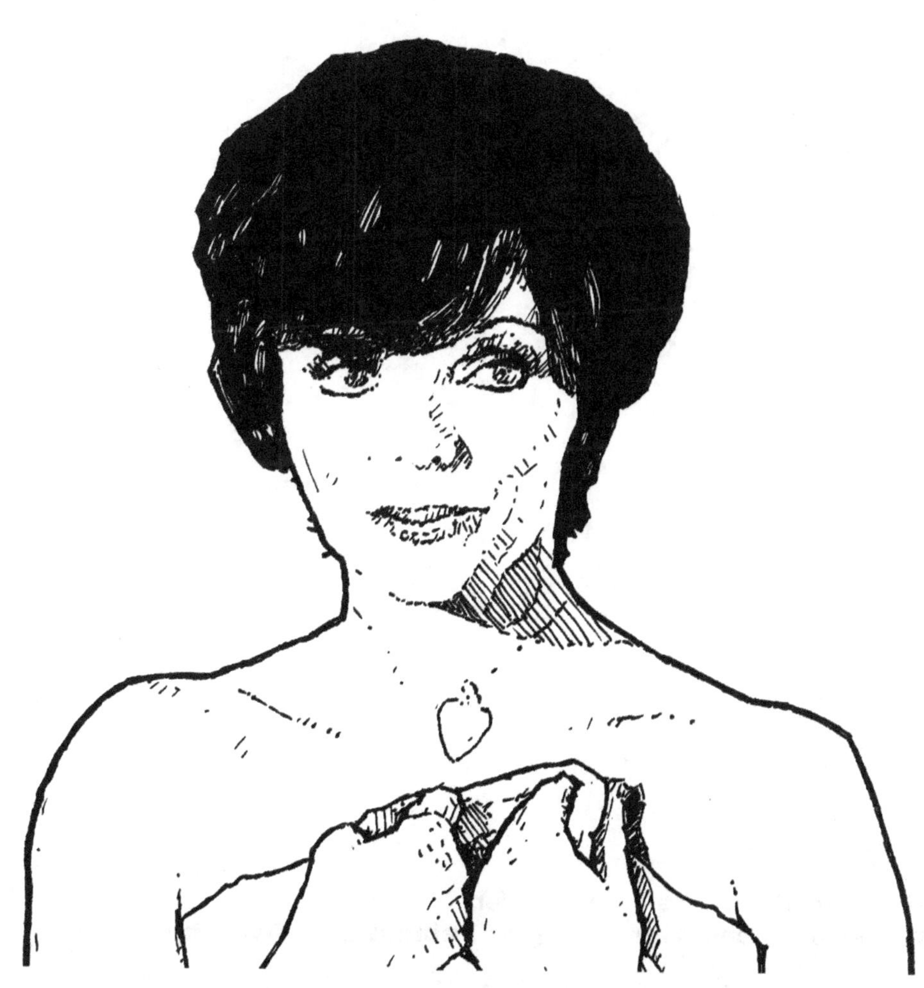

Jerry Stiller (born Gerald Isaac Stiller)
as Lt. Rico Patrone, **The Taking of Pelham One Two Three** (1974)

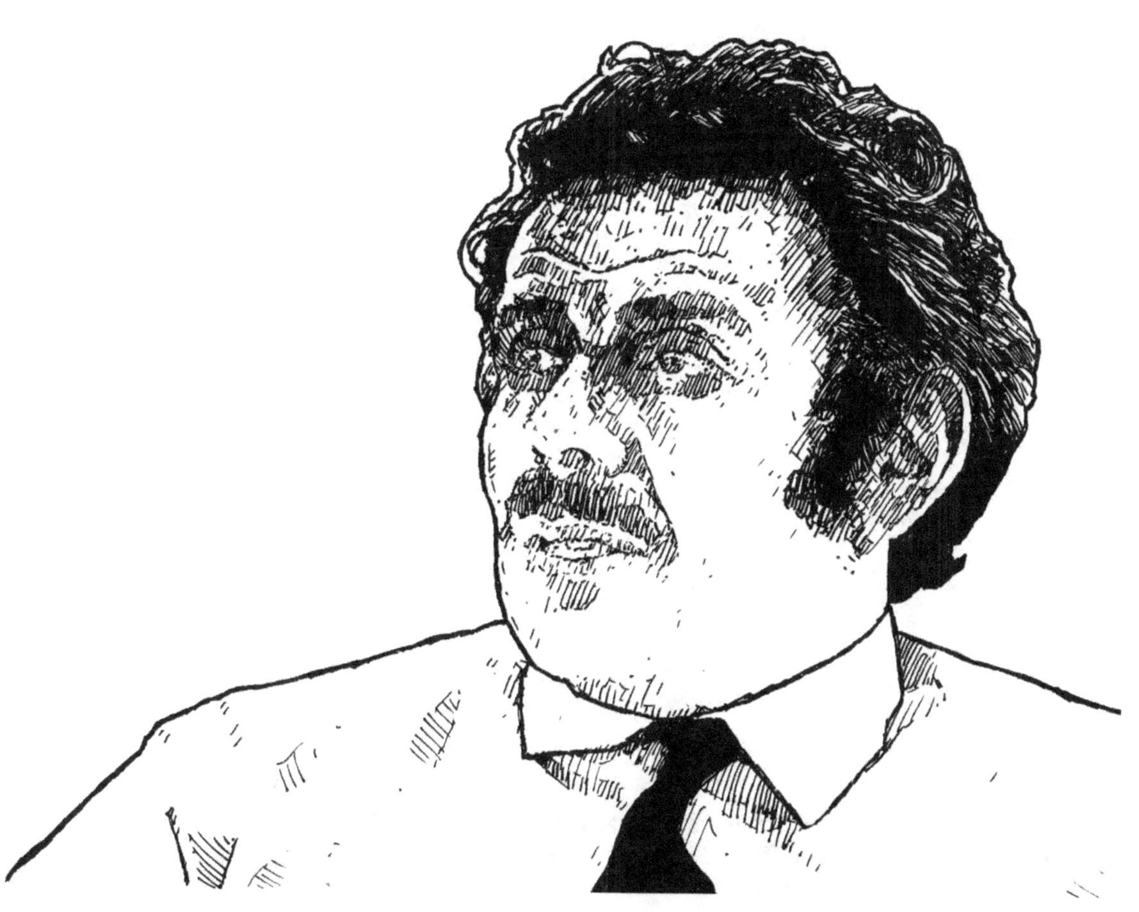

Bernadette Peters (born Bernadette Lazzara)
as the Warden's Secretary, **The Longest Yard** (1974)

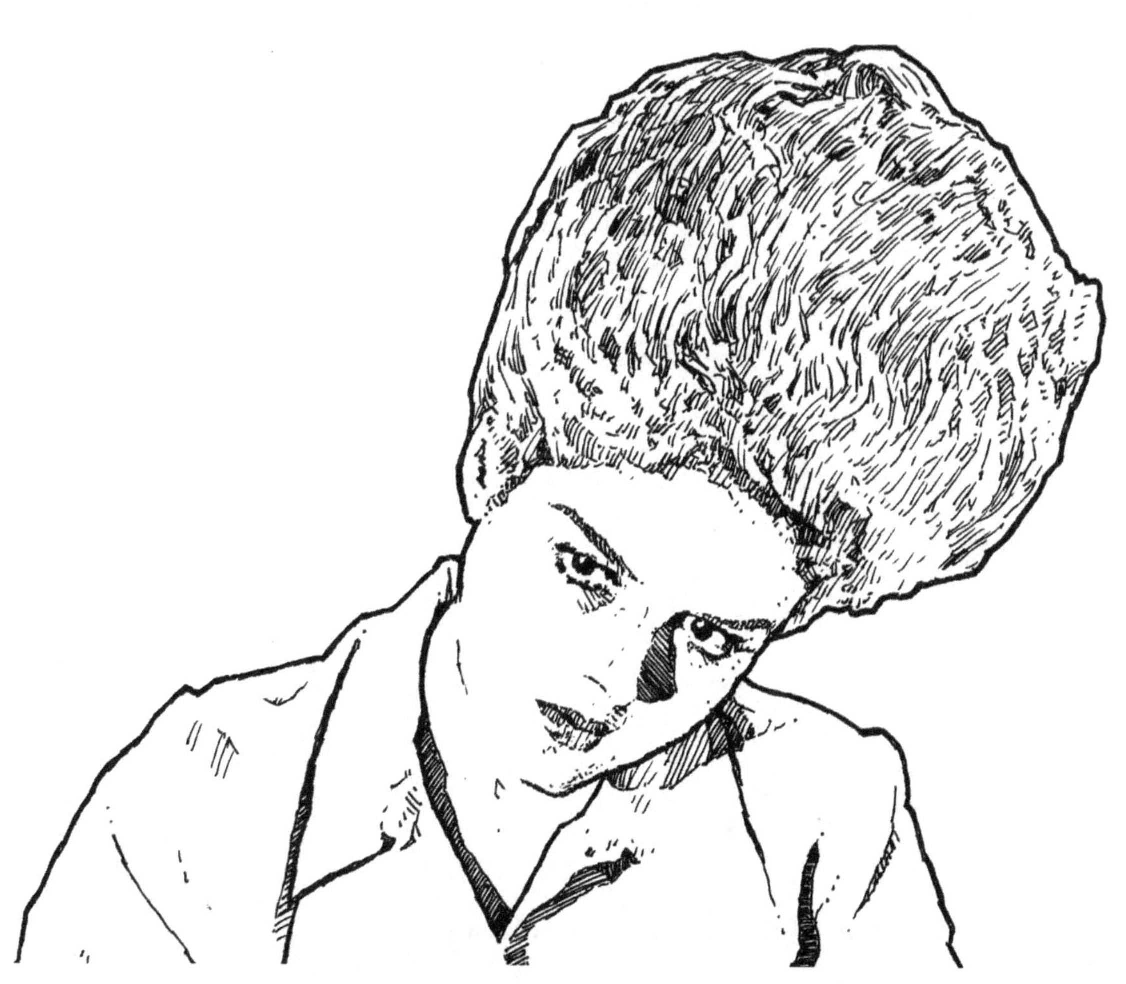

Abe Vigoda as as John Dellanzia, **Newman's Law** (1974)

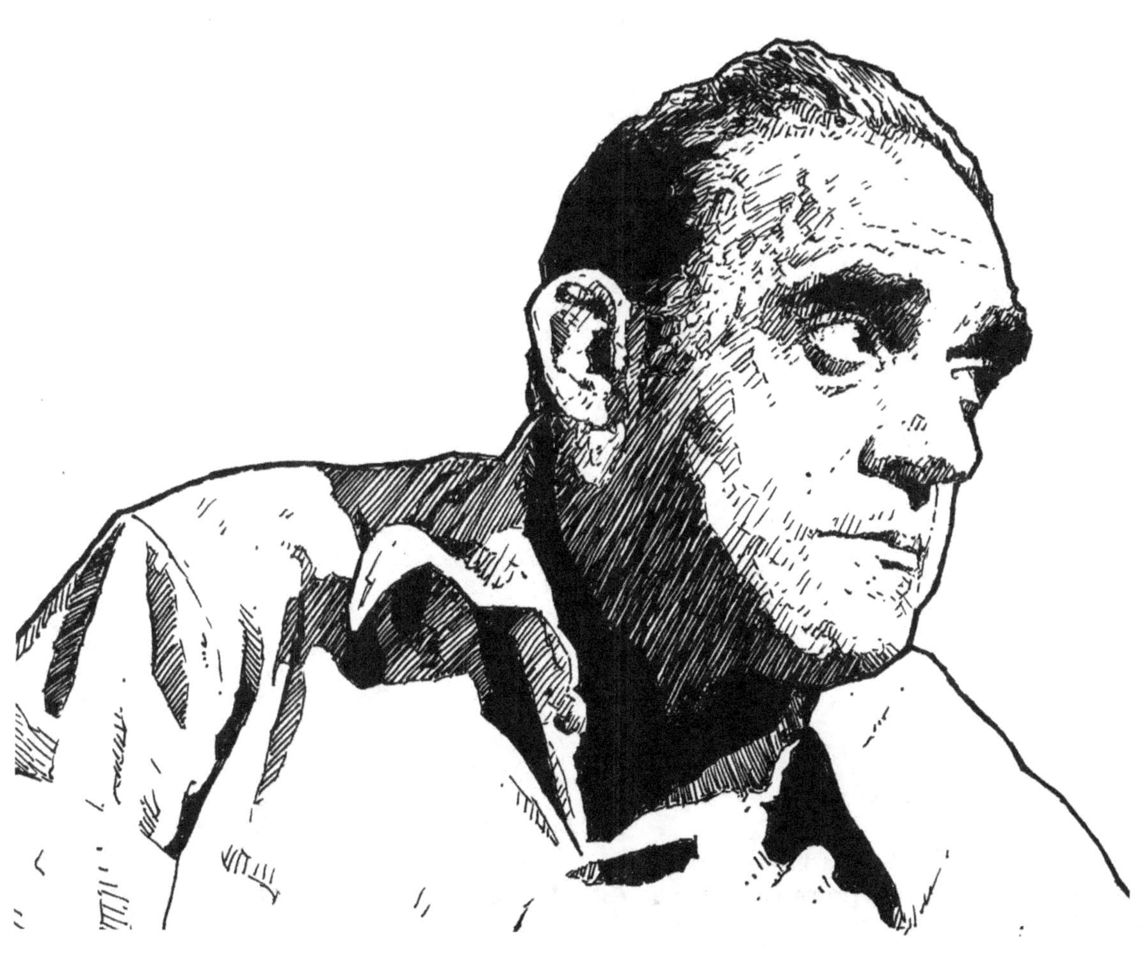

Ringo Starr (born Richard Starkey)
as Pope Gregory XVI (born Bartolomeo Alberto Cappellari), **Lisztomania** (1975)

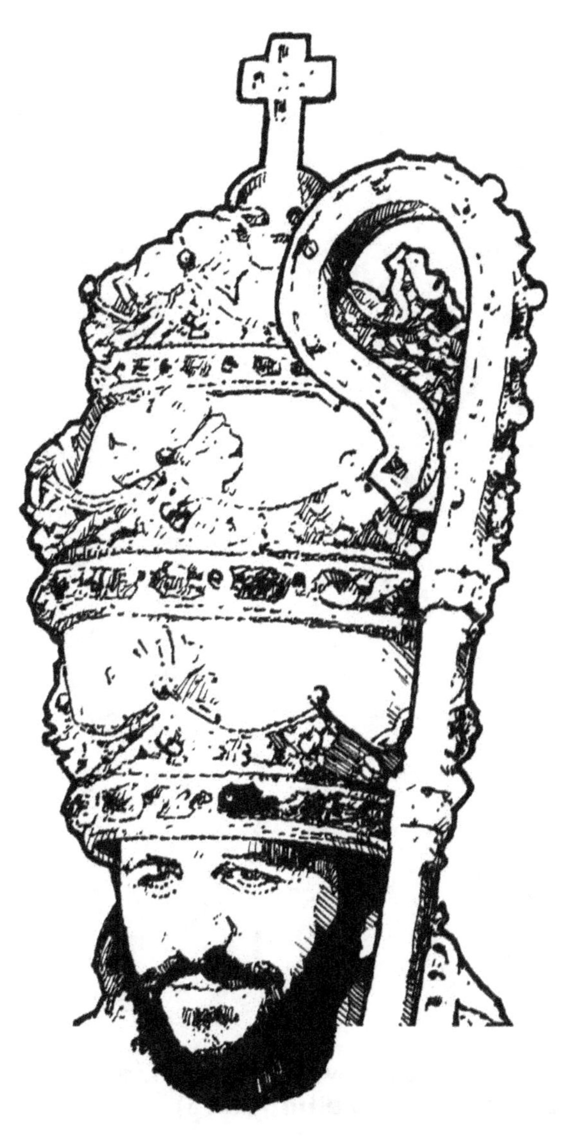

Donald Sutherland
as Giacomo Girolamo Casanova, **Fellini's Casanova**
[Il Casanova di Federico Fellini] (1976)

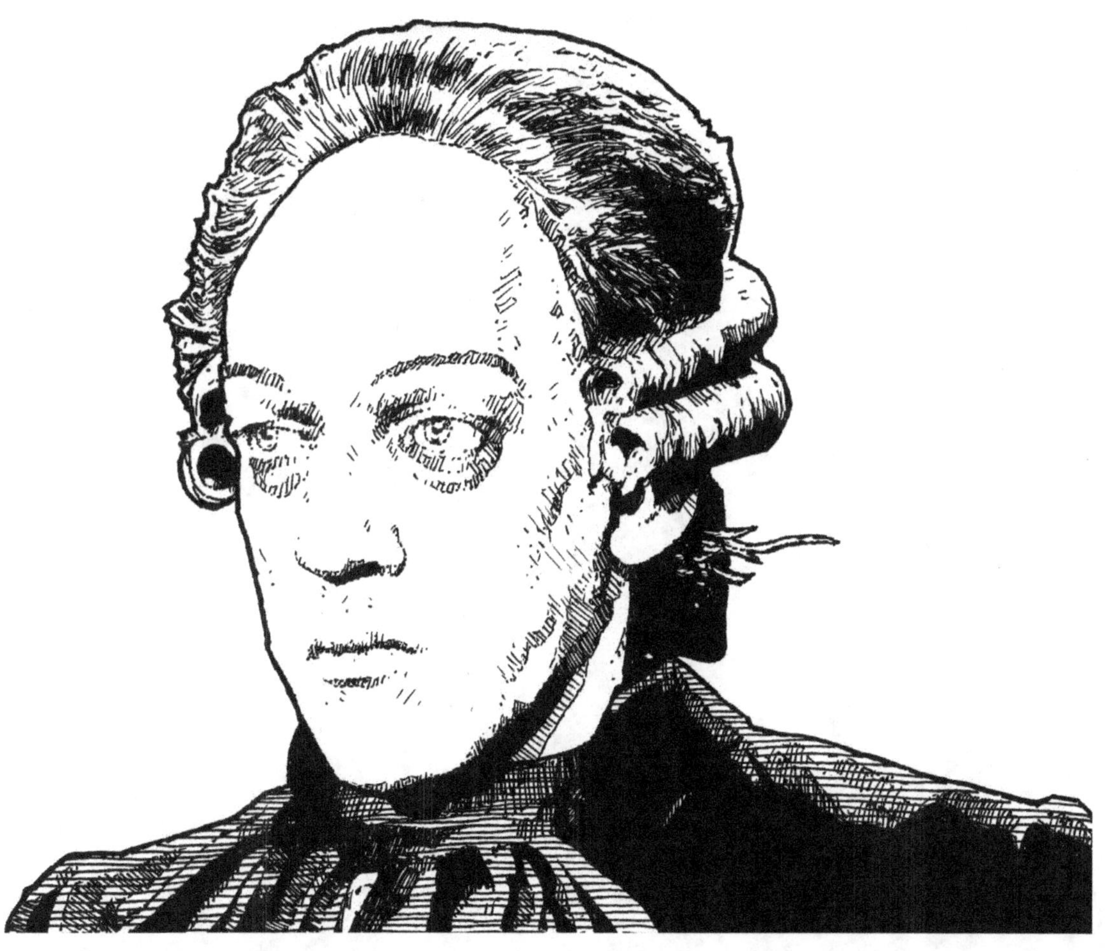

Joe Dallesandro (born Joseph Angelo D'Allesandro III)
as Krassky, **Je t'aime moi non plus** (1976)

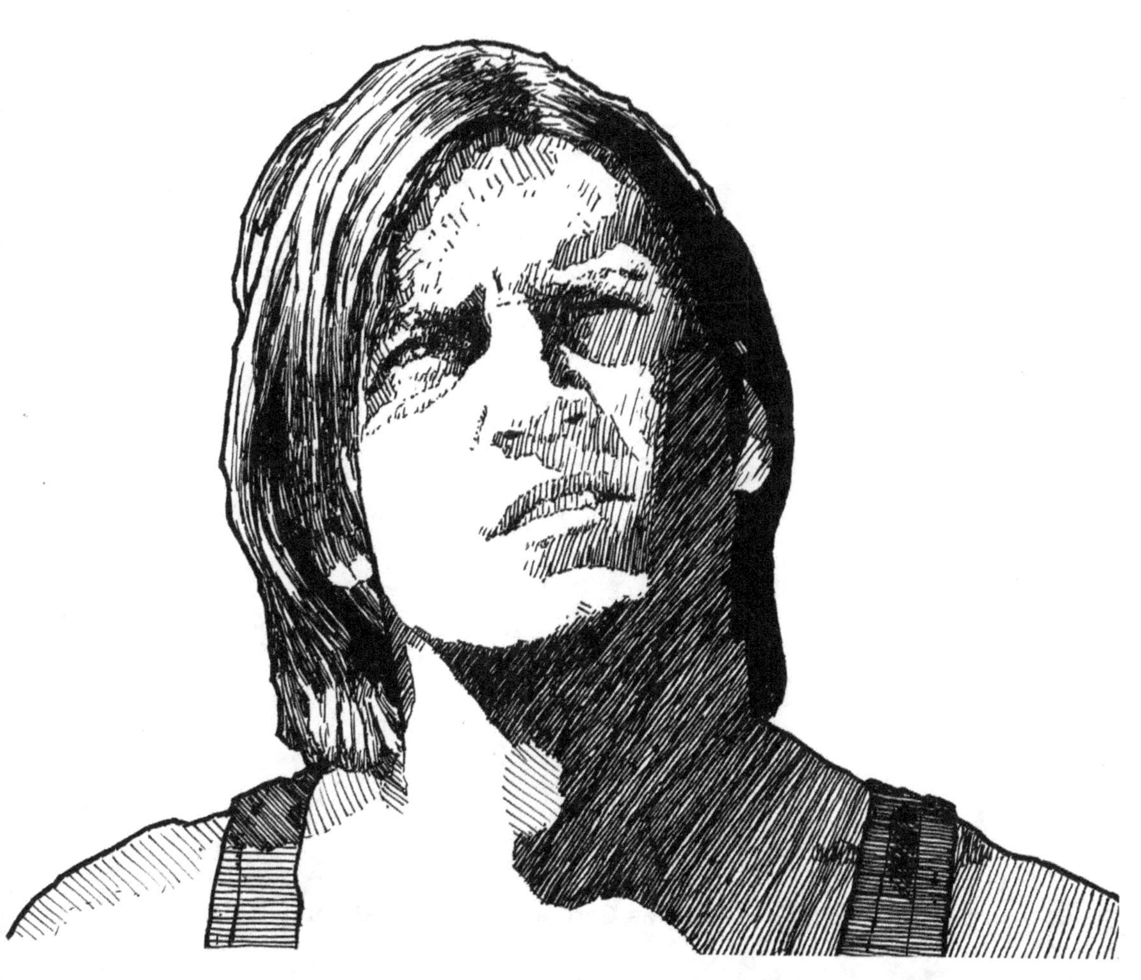

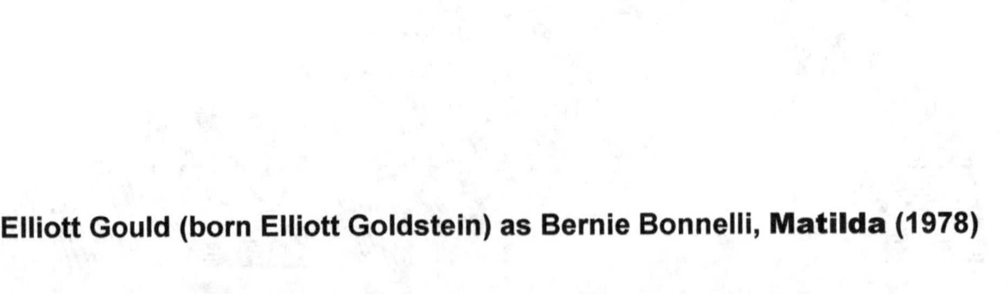

Elliott Gould (born Elliott Goldstein) as Bernie Bonnelli, **Matilda** (1978)

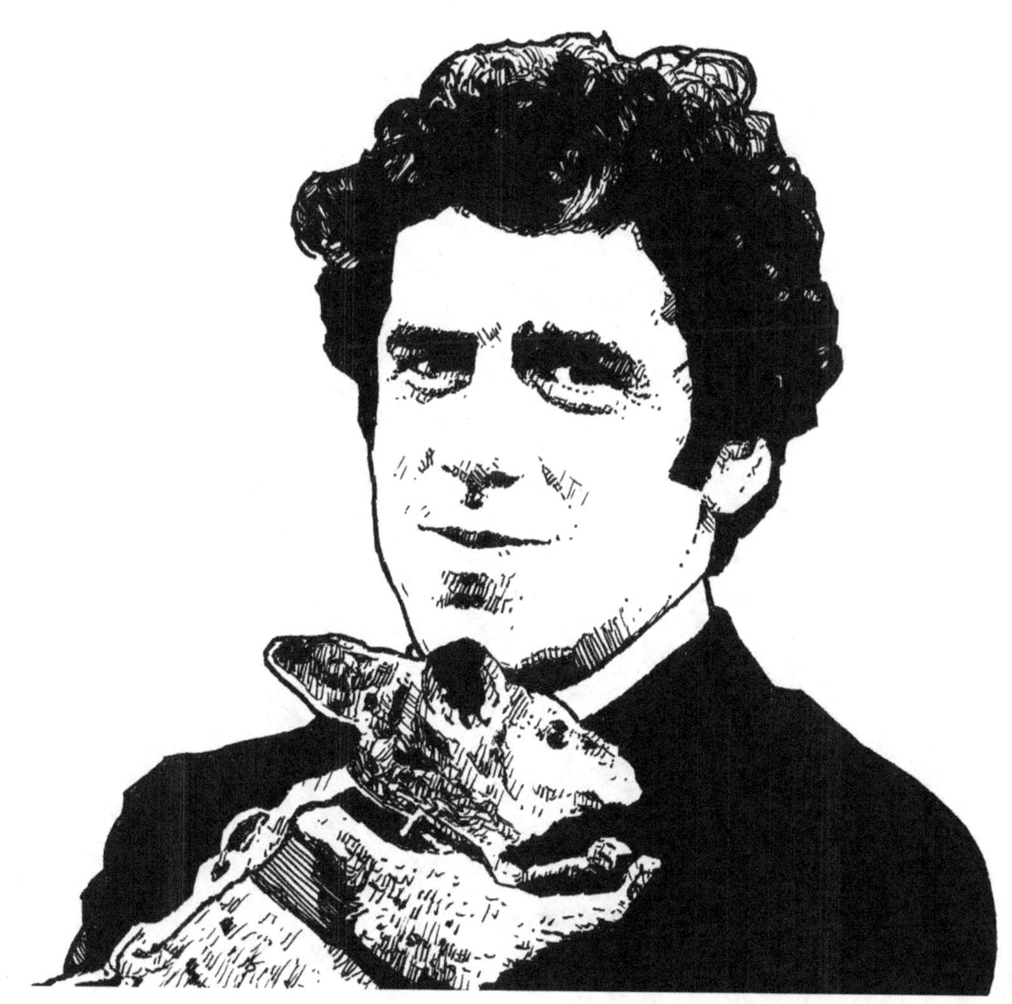

Dennis Christopher (born Dennis Carrelli)
as Dave Stohler (as Enrico Gimondi), **Breaking Away** (1979)

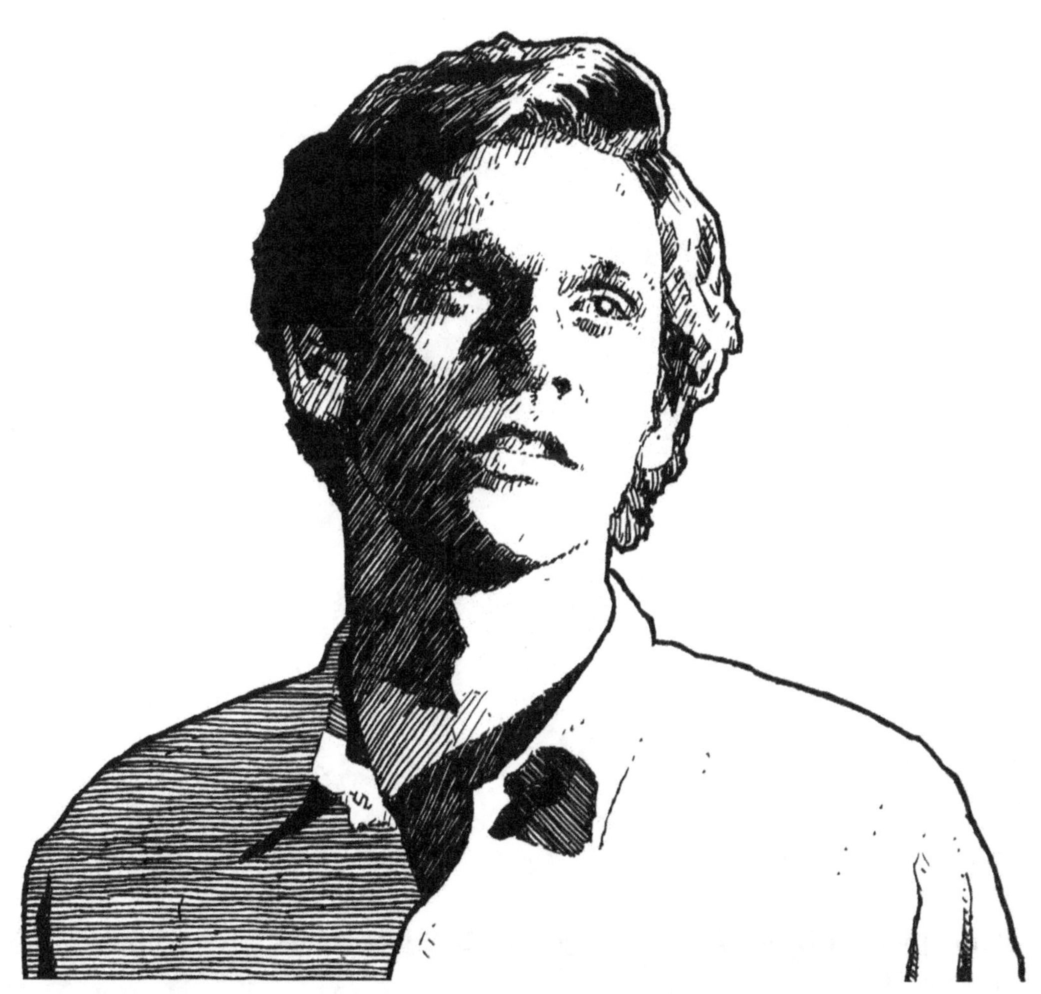

Peter O'Toole as Tiberius Caesar Augustus, **Caligula** (1979)

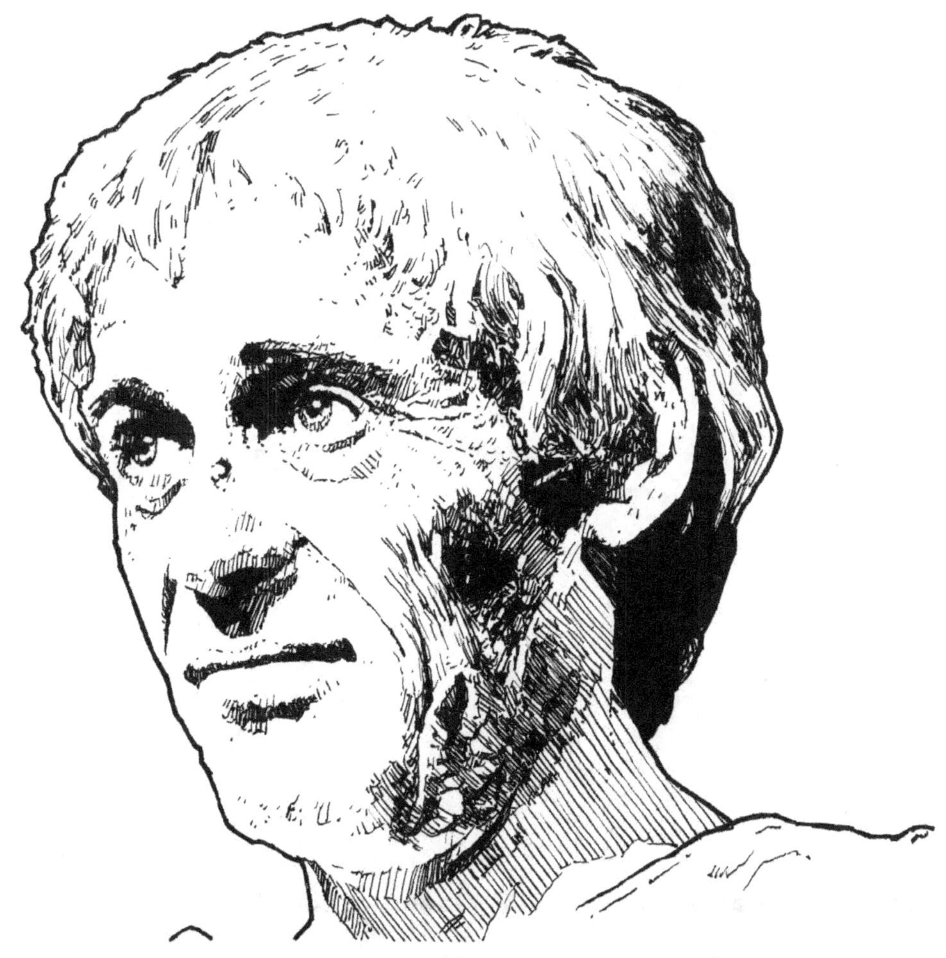

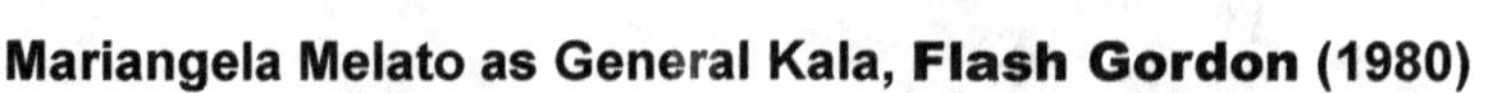

Mariangela Melato as General Kala, Flash Gordon (1980)

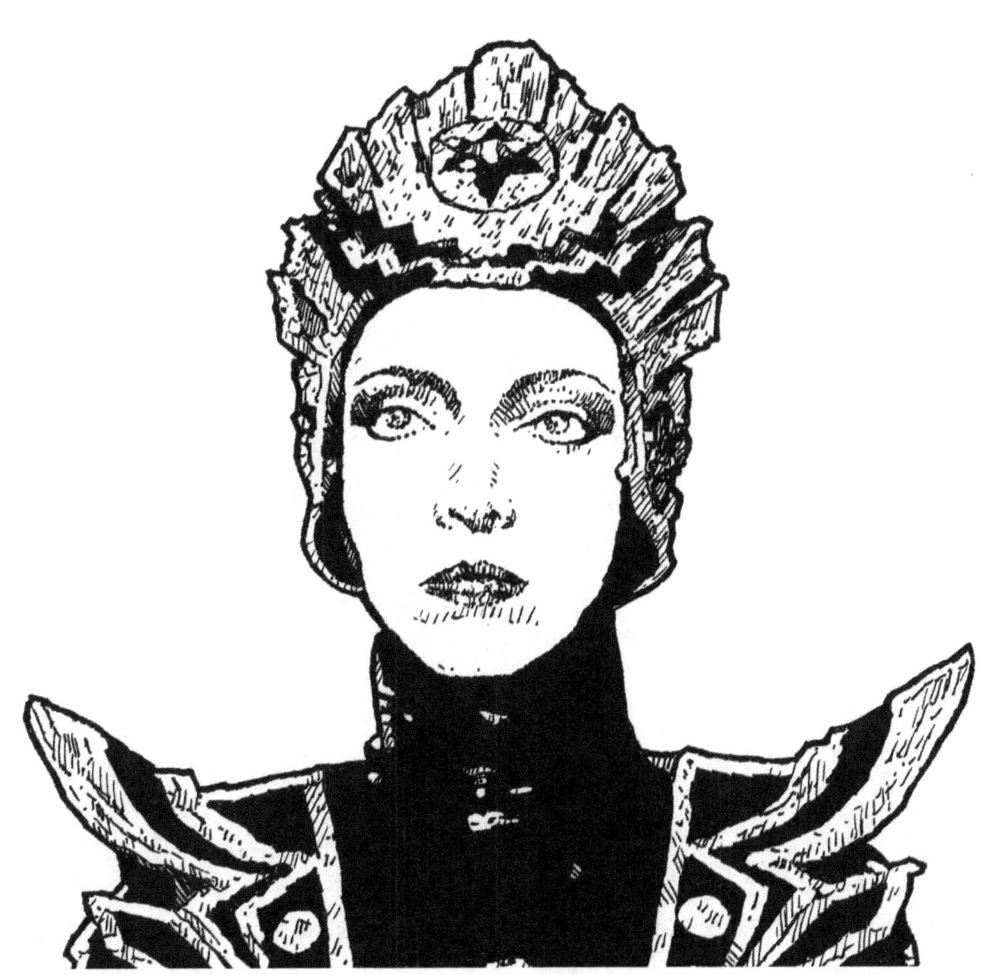

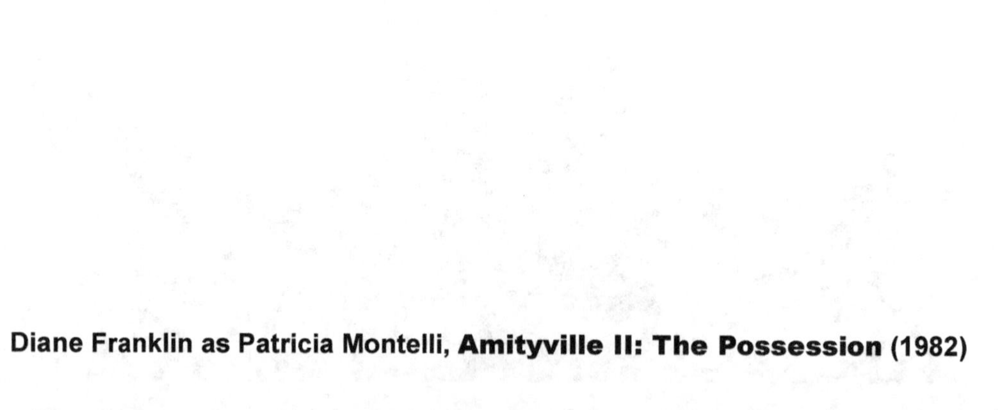
Diane Franklin as Patricia Montelli, **Amityville II: The Possession** (1982)

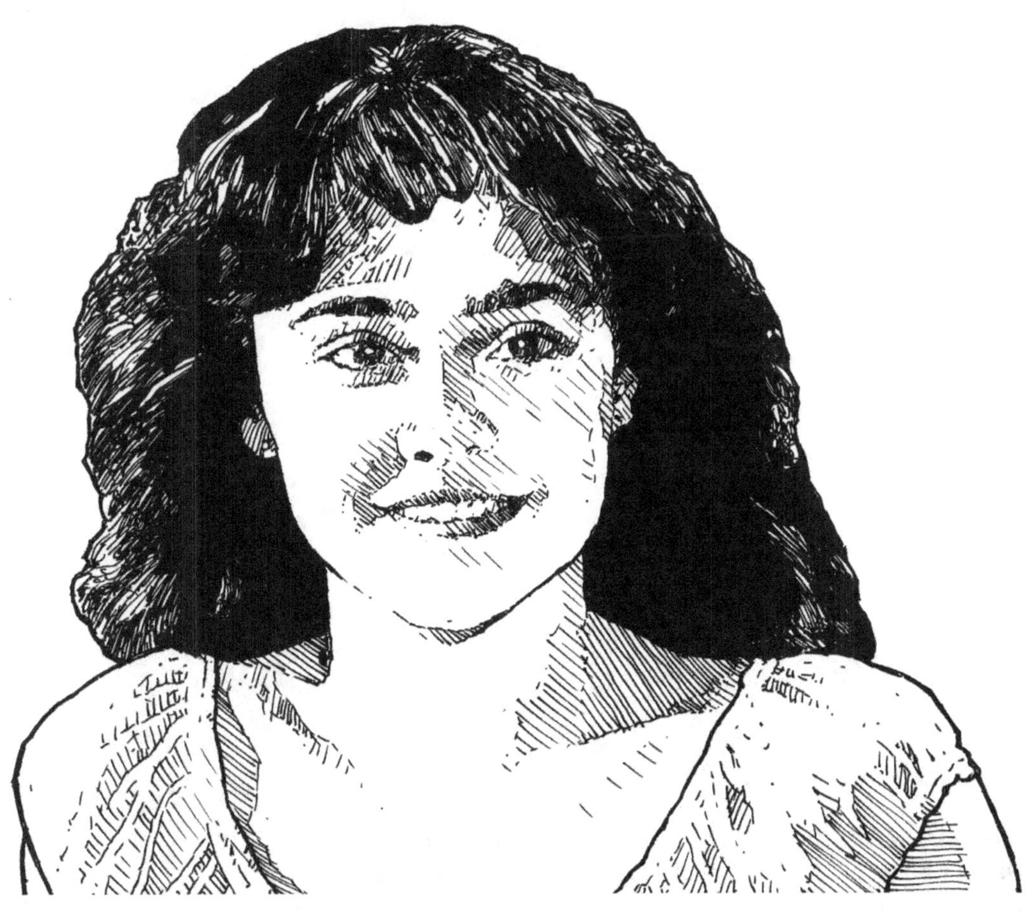

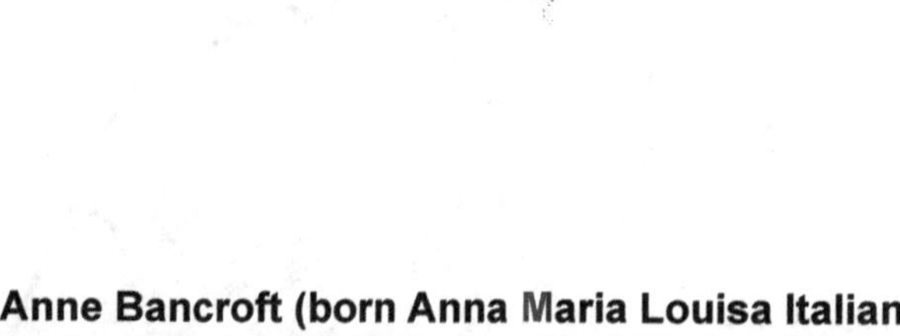
Anne Bancroft (born Anna Maria Louisa Italiano) as Anna Bronski, **To Be or Not To Be** (1983)

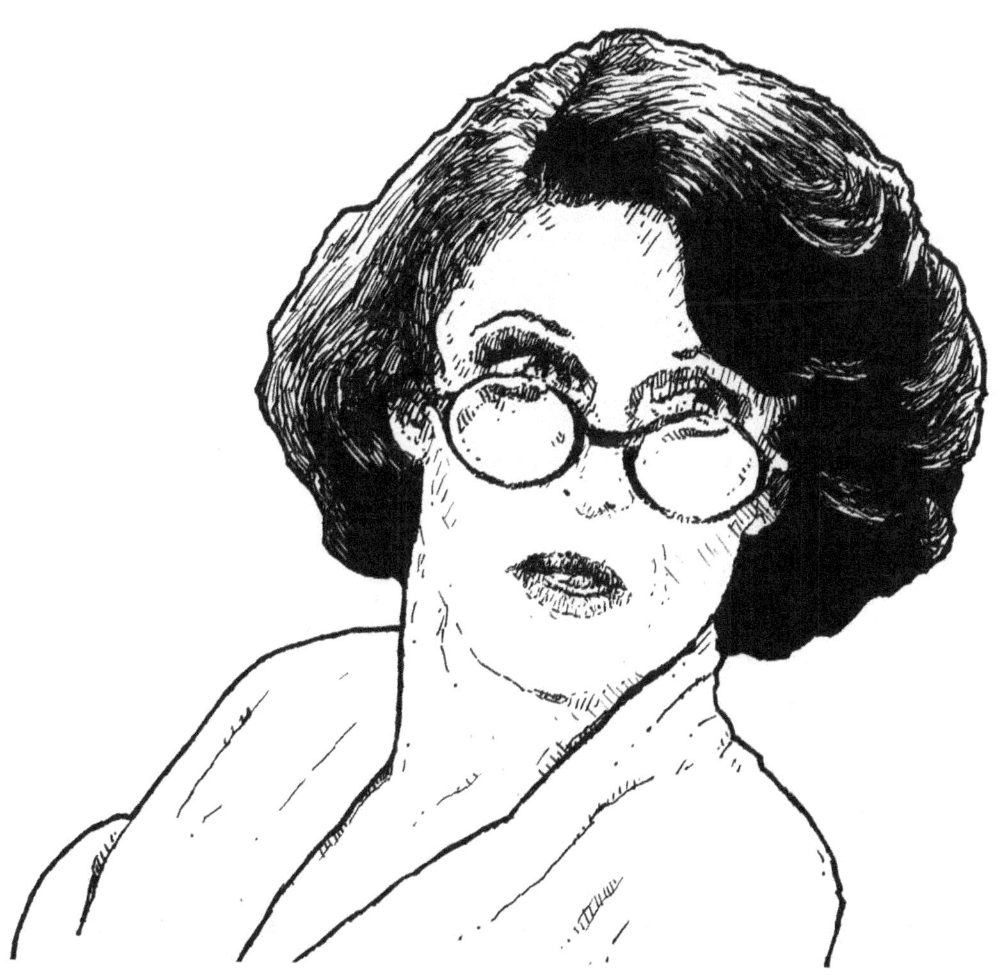

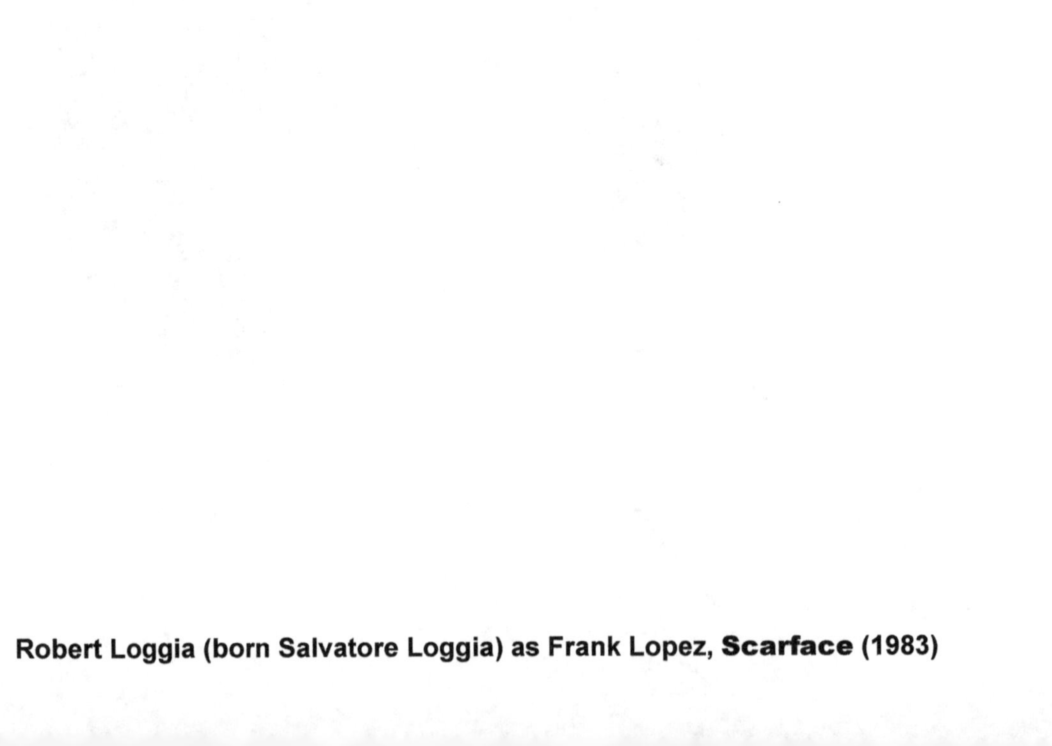

Robert Loggia (born Salvatore Loggia) as Frank Lopez, **Scarface** (1983)

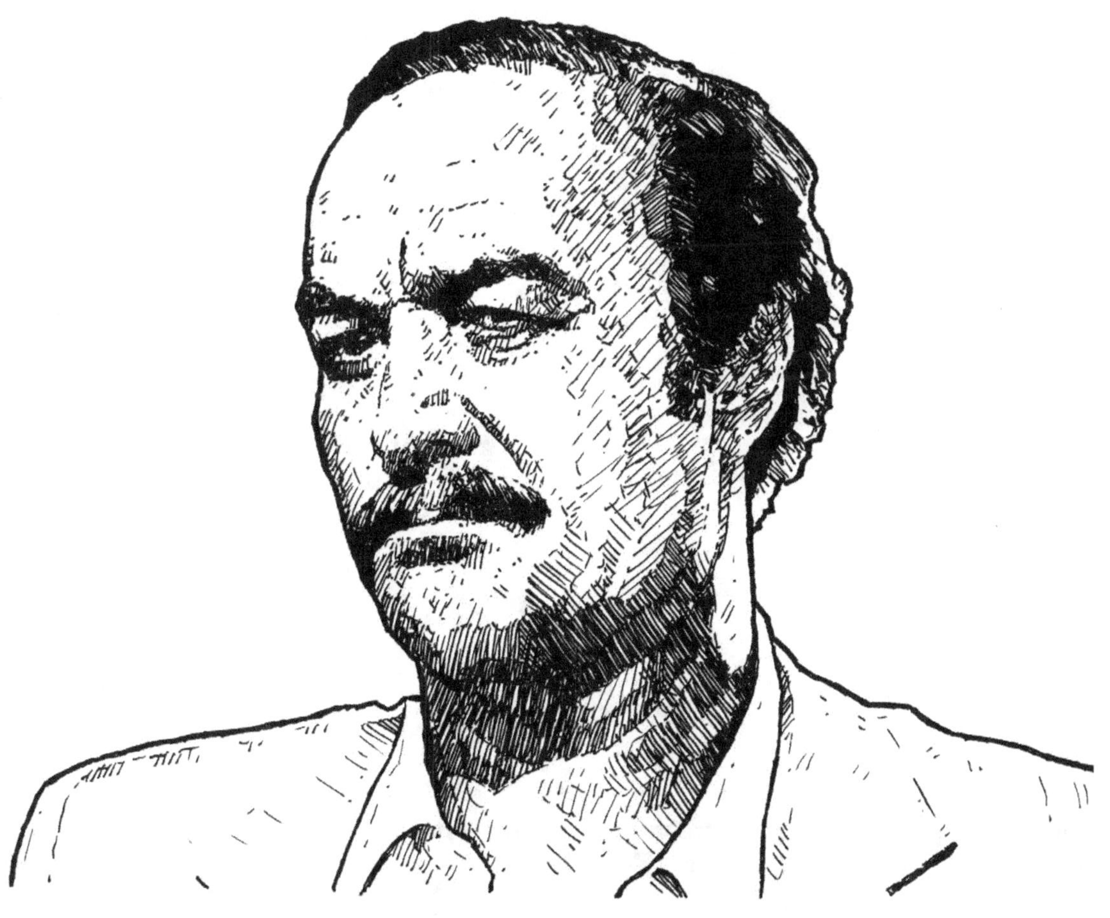

Mia Farrow (born María de Lourdes Villiers Farrow)
as Tina Vitale, **Broadway Danny Rose** (1984)

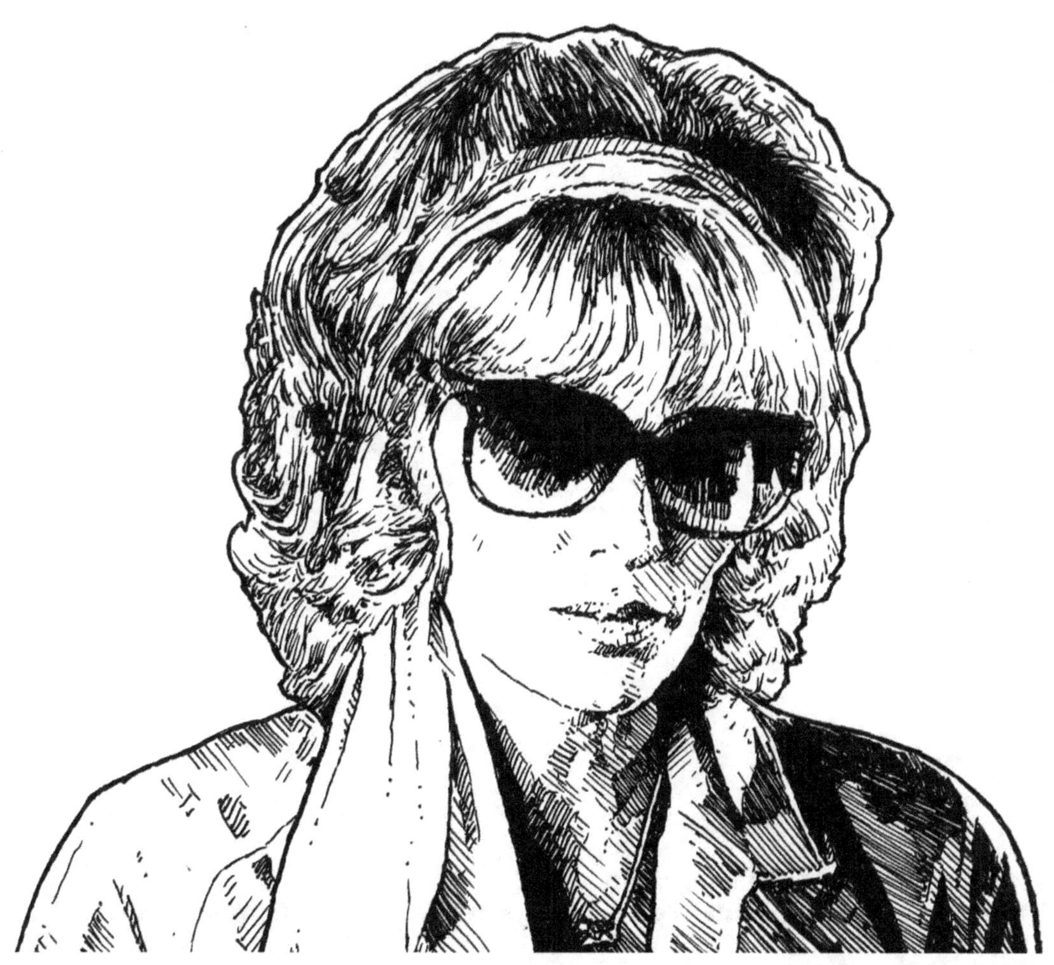

John Lithgow as Dr. Emilio Lizardo,
The Adventures of Buckaroo Banzai Across the 8th Dimension (1984)

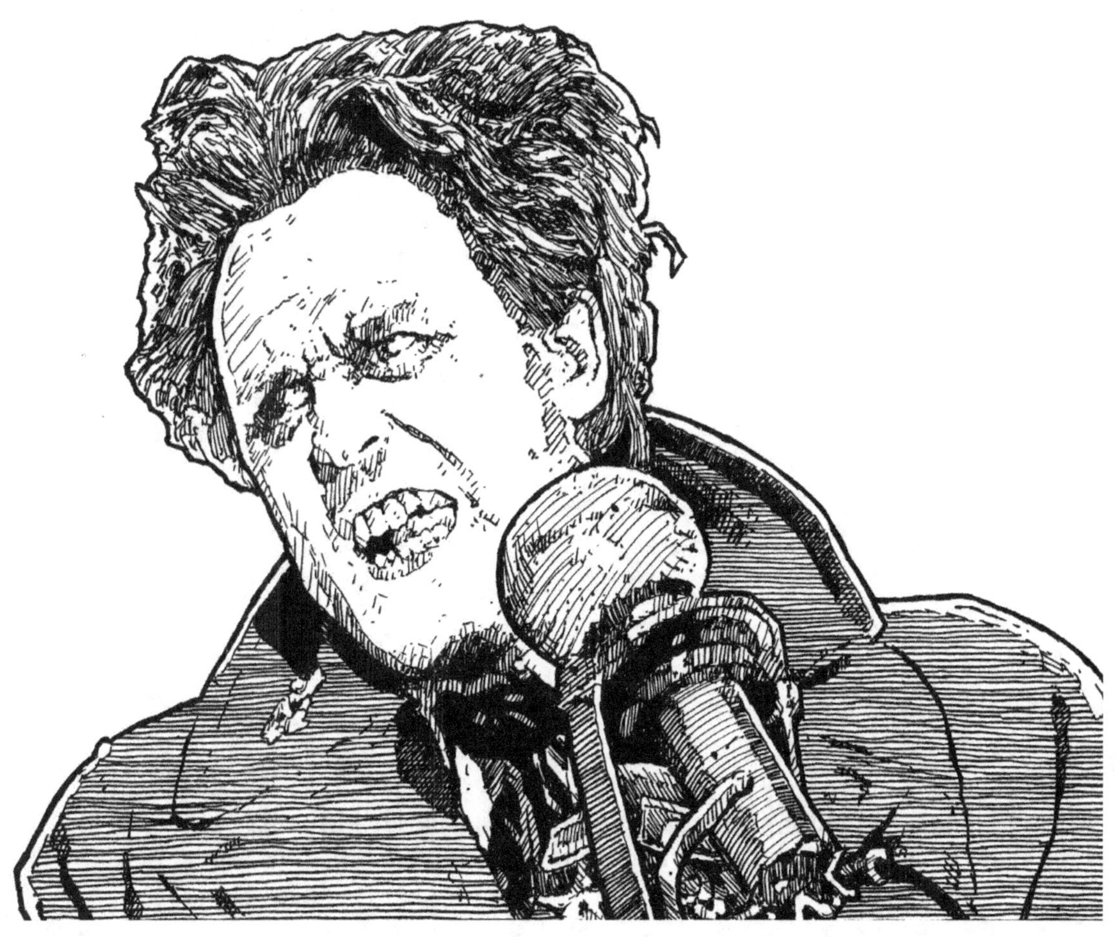

Jack Nicholson (born John Joseph Nicholson) as Charley Partanna,
John Randolph (born Emanuel Hirsch Cohen) as Angelo "Pop" Partanna,
Prizzi's Honor (1985)

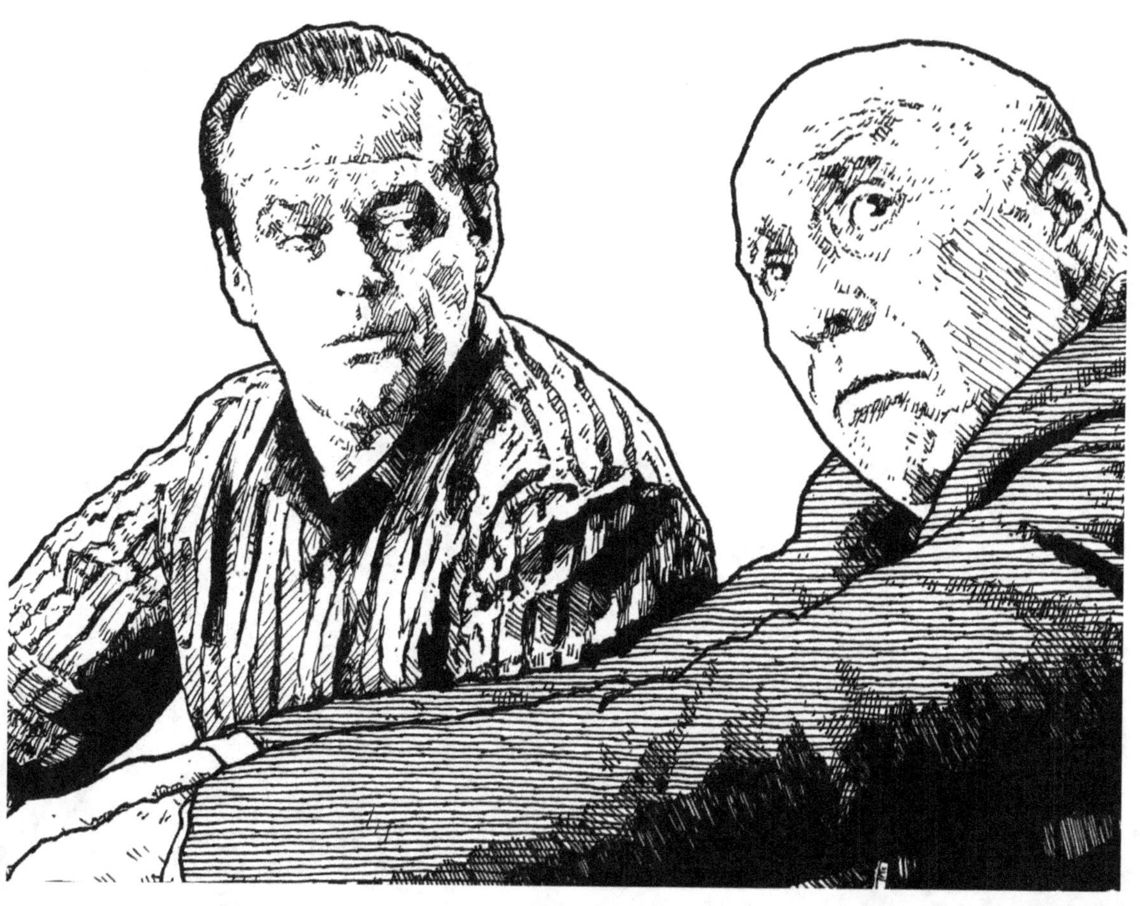

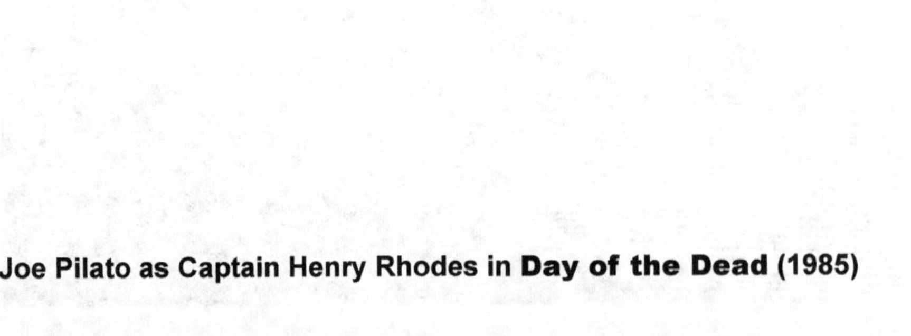

Joe Pilato as Captain Henry Rhodes in **Day of the Dead** (1985)

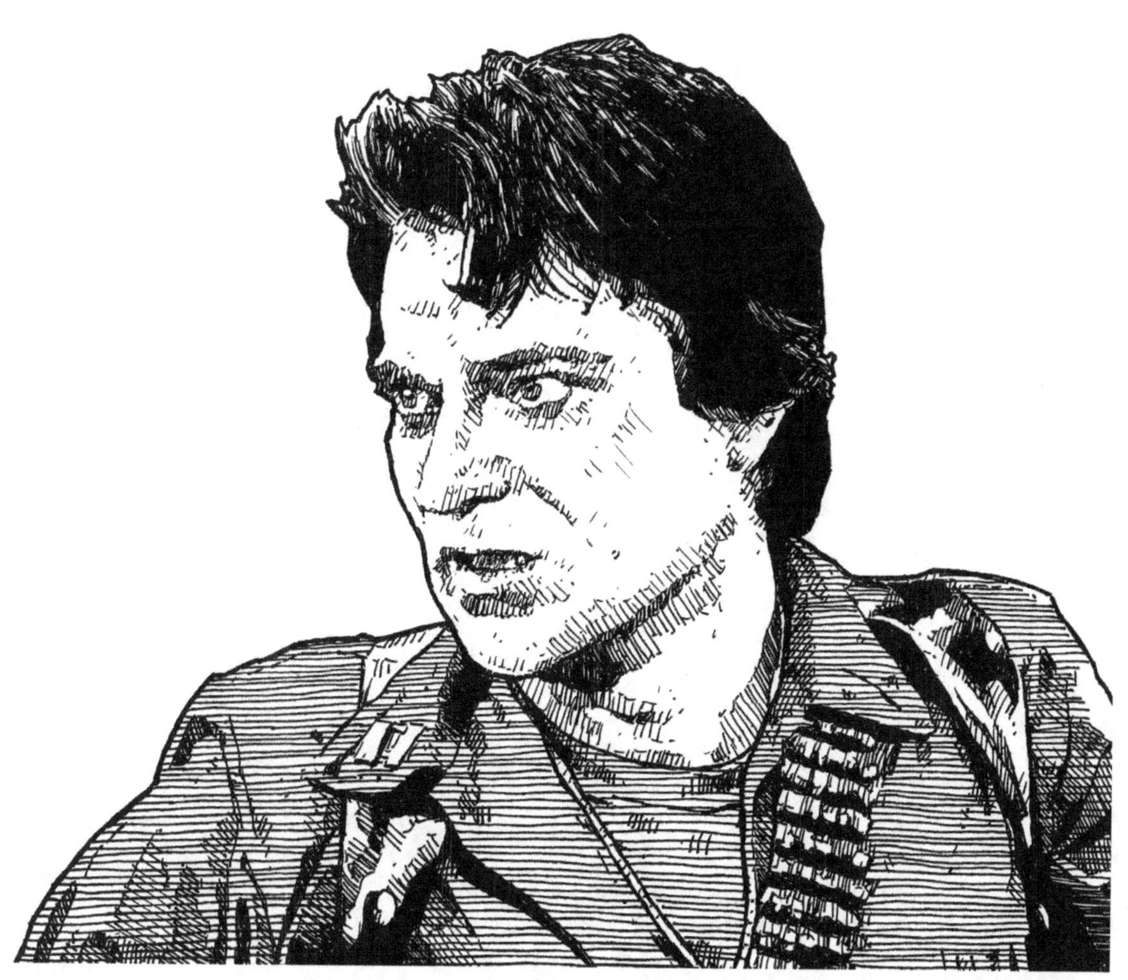

Vincent Gardenia (born Vincenzo Gardenia Scognamiglio)
as Mushnik, **Little Shop of Horrors** (1986)

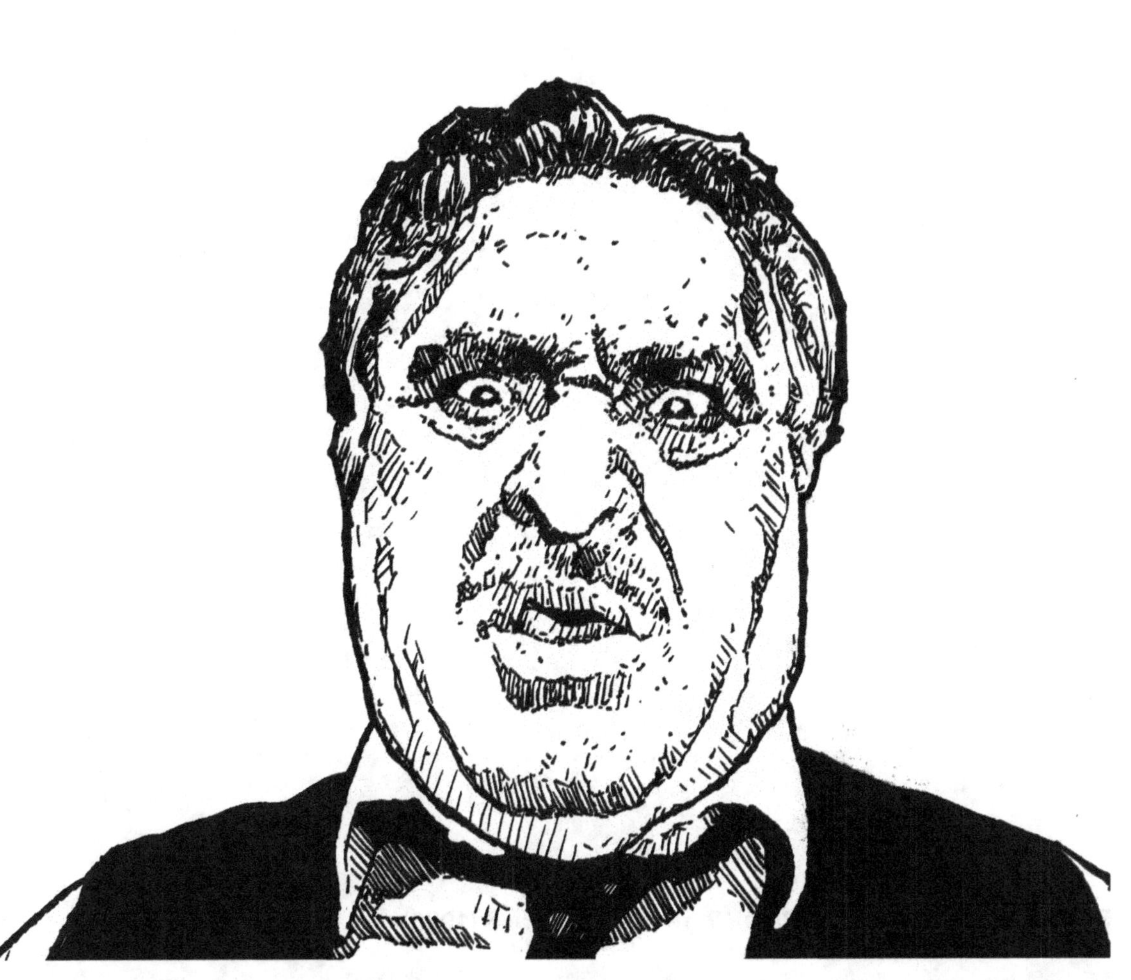

Robert Forster as Abdul Rafai, **The Delta Force** (1986)

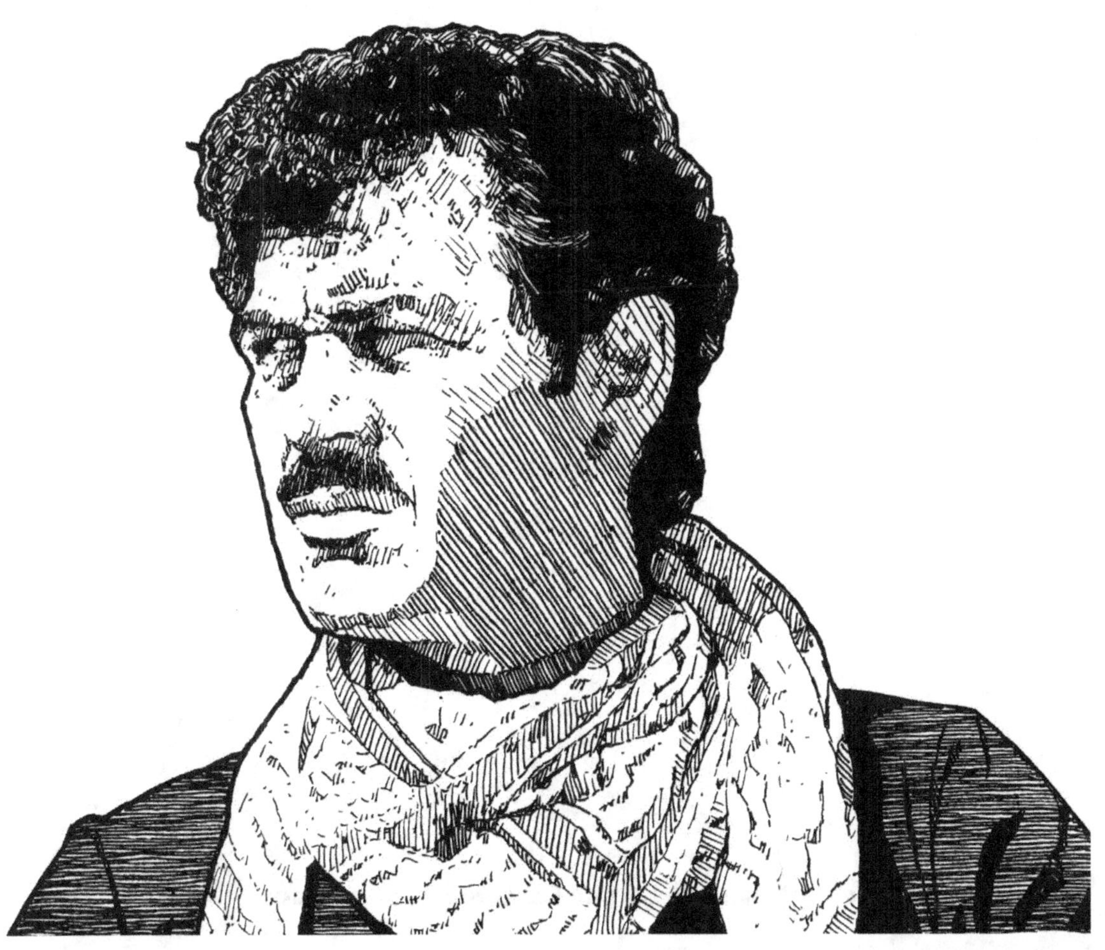

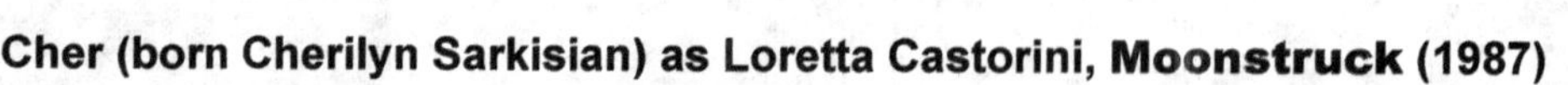

Cher (born Cherilyn Sarkisian) as Loretta Castorini, **Moonstruck** (1987)

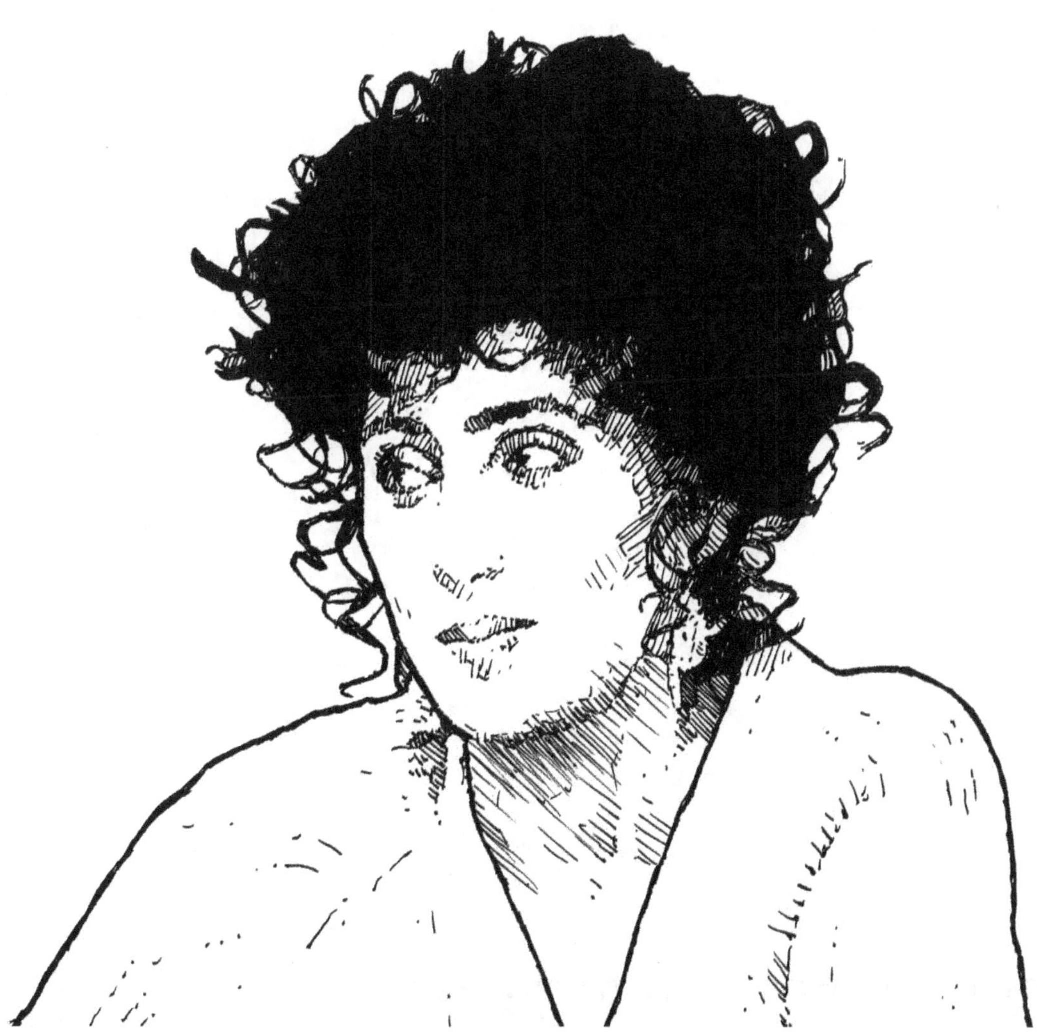

Terence Stamp as Prince Borsa, **The Sicilian** (1987)

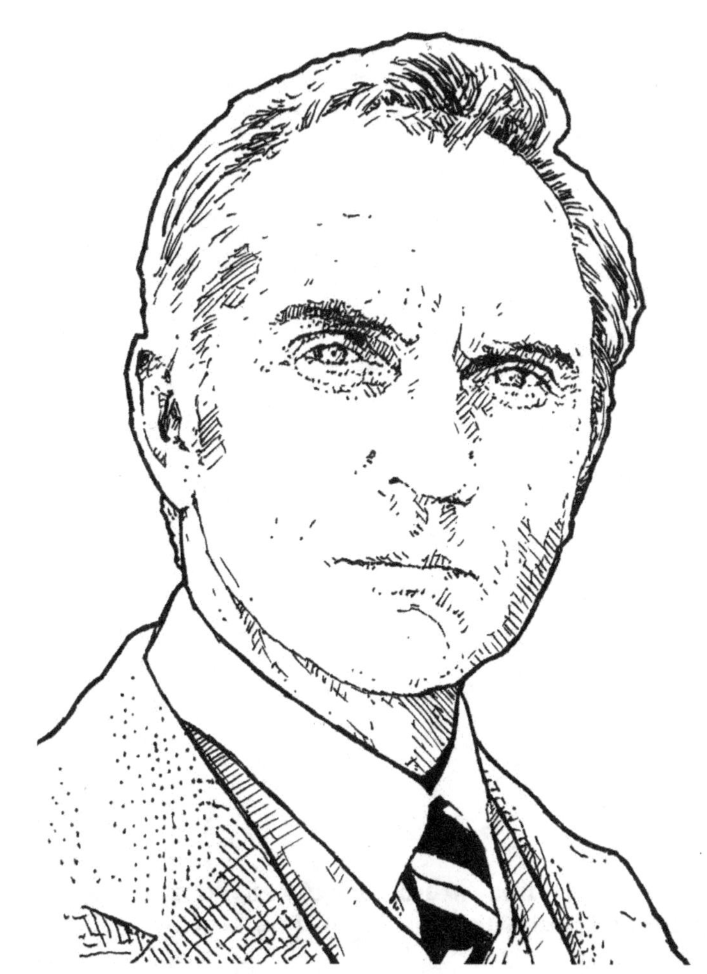

Andy Garcia (born Andrés Arturo García Menéndez)
as George Stone (born Giuseppe Petri), **The Untouchables** (1987)

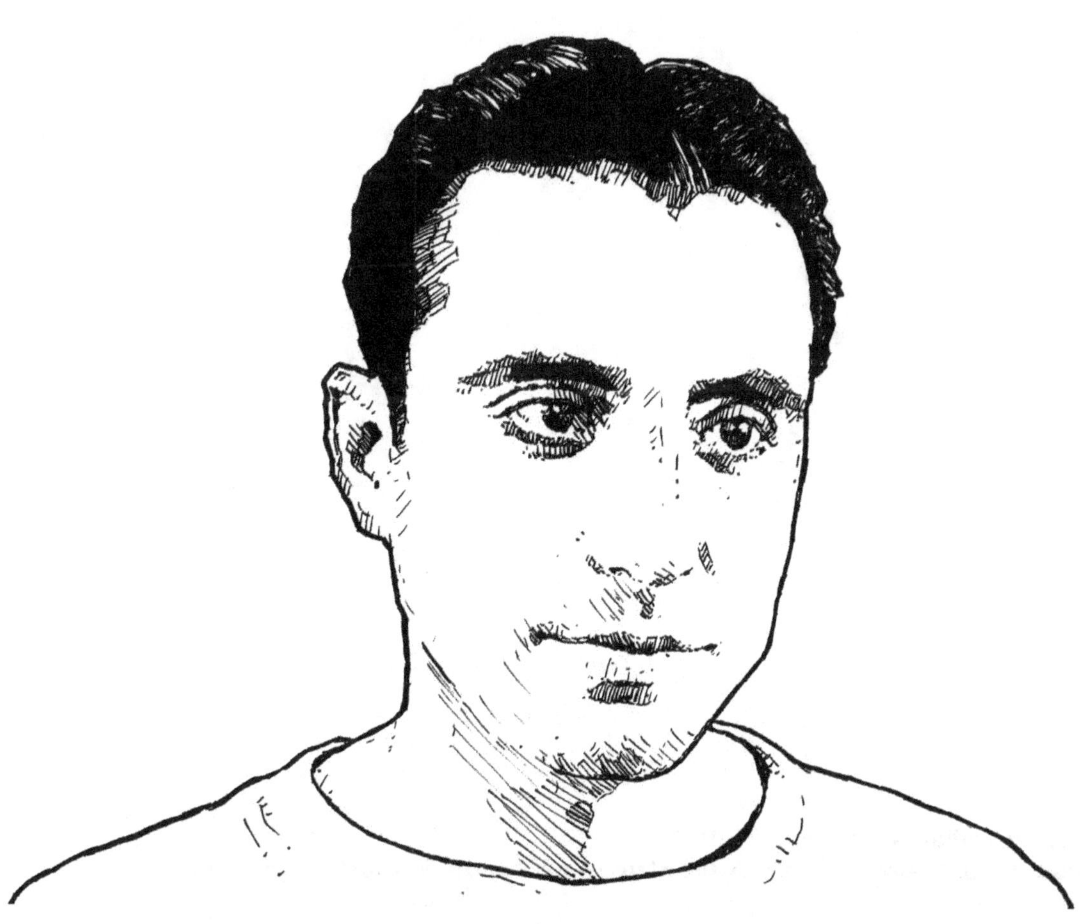

Robin Williams (as Ray D. Tutto)
as King of the Moon, **The Adventures of Baron Munchausen (1988)**

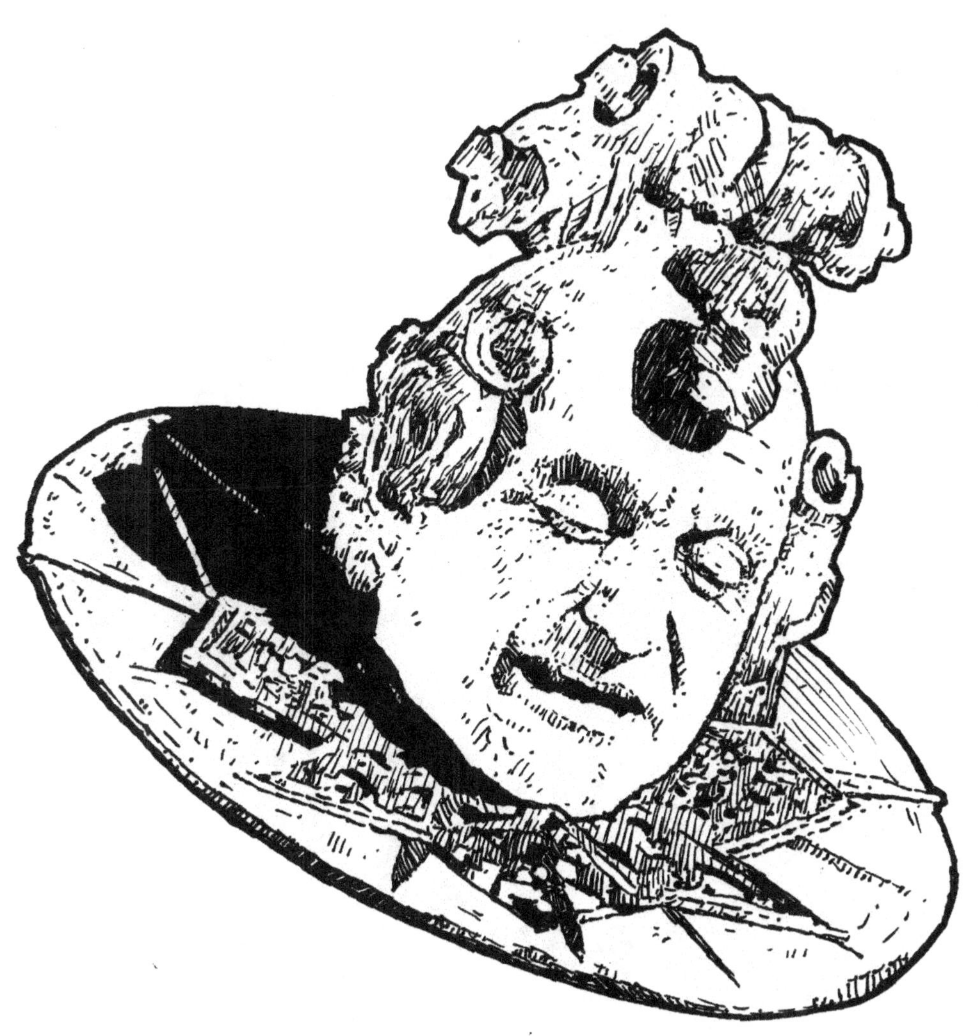

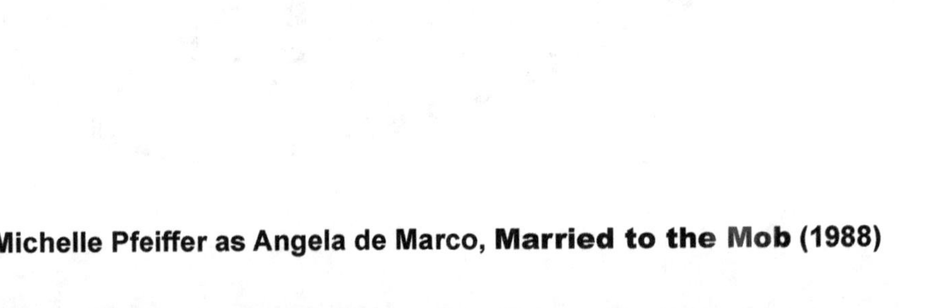

Michelle Pfeiffer as Angela de Marco, Married to the Mob (1988)

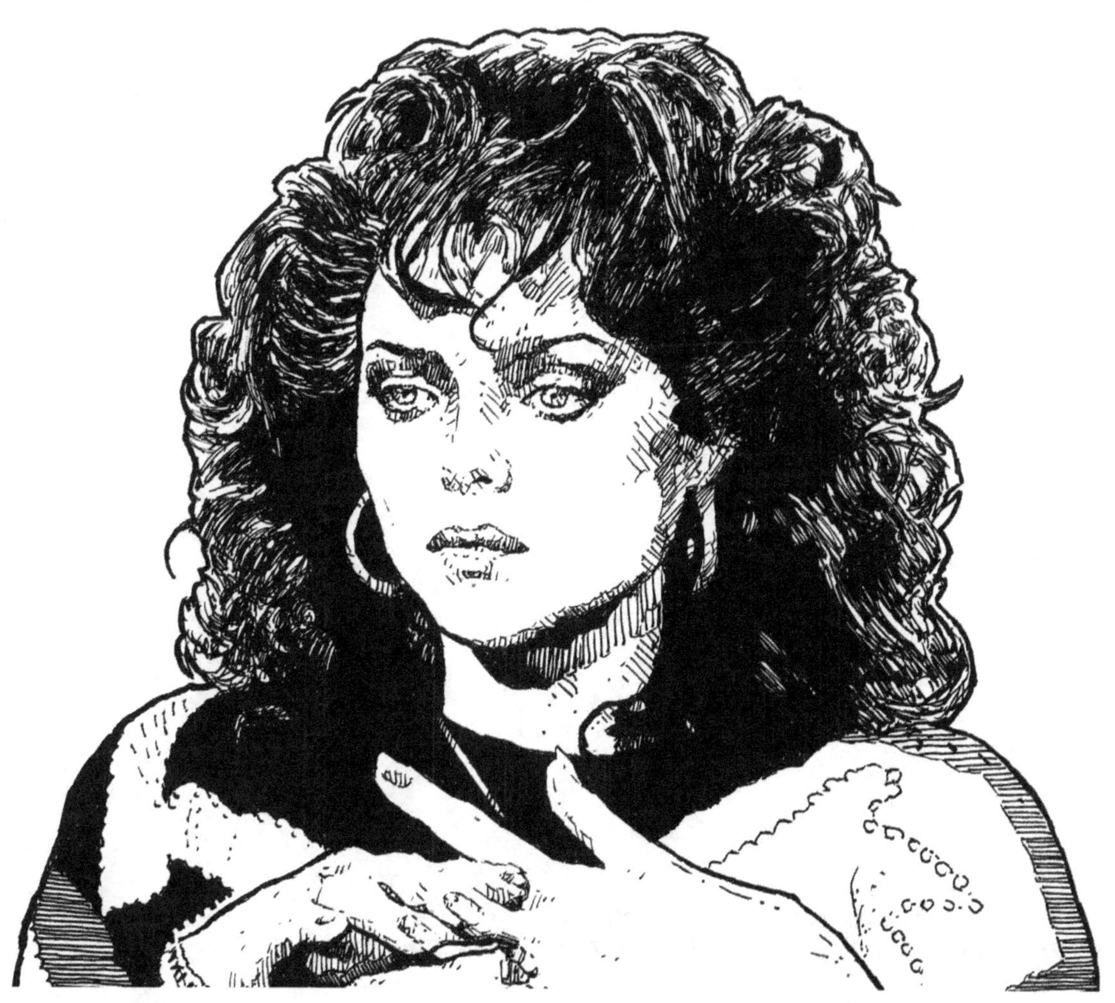

Walter Matthau (born Walter John Matthow)
as Padre Maurizio, **Il piccolo diavolo [The Little Devil]** (1988)

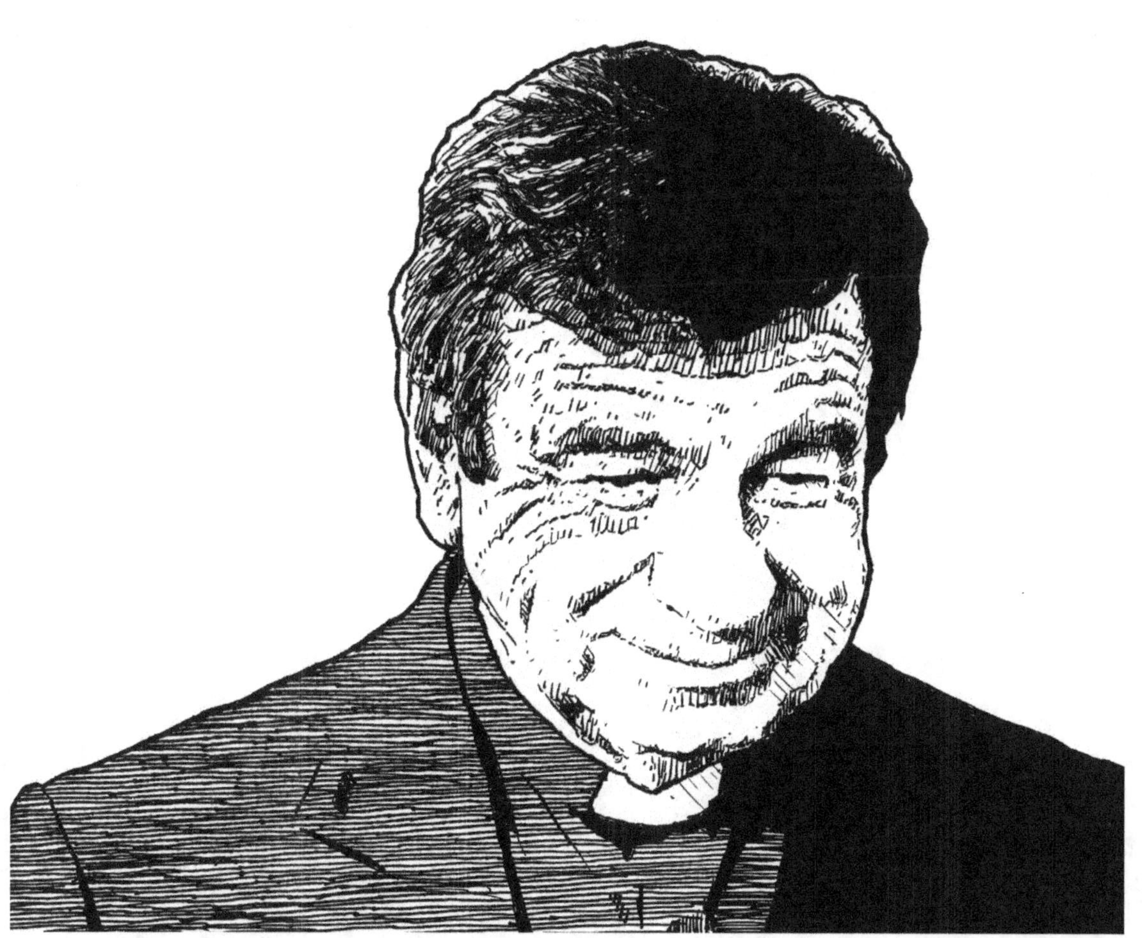

Sonny Bono (born Salvatore Phillip Bono) as Franklin von Tussle, **Hairspray** (1988)

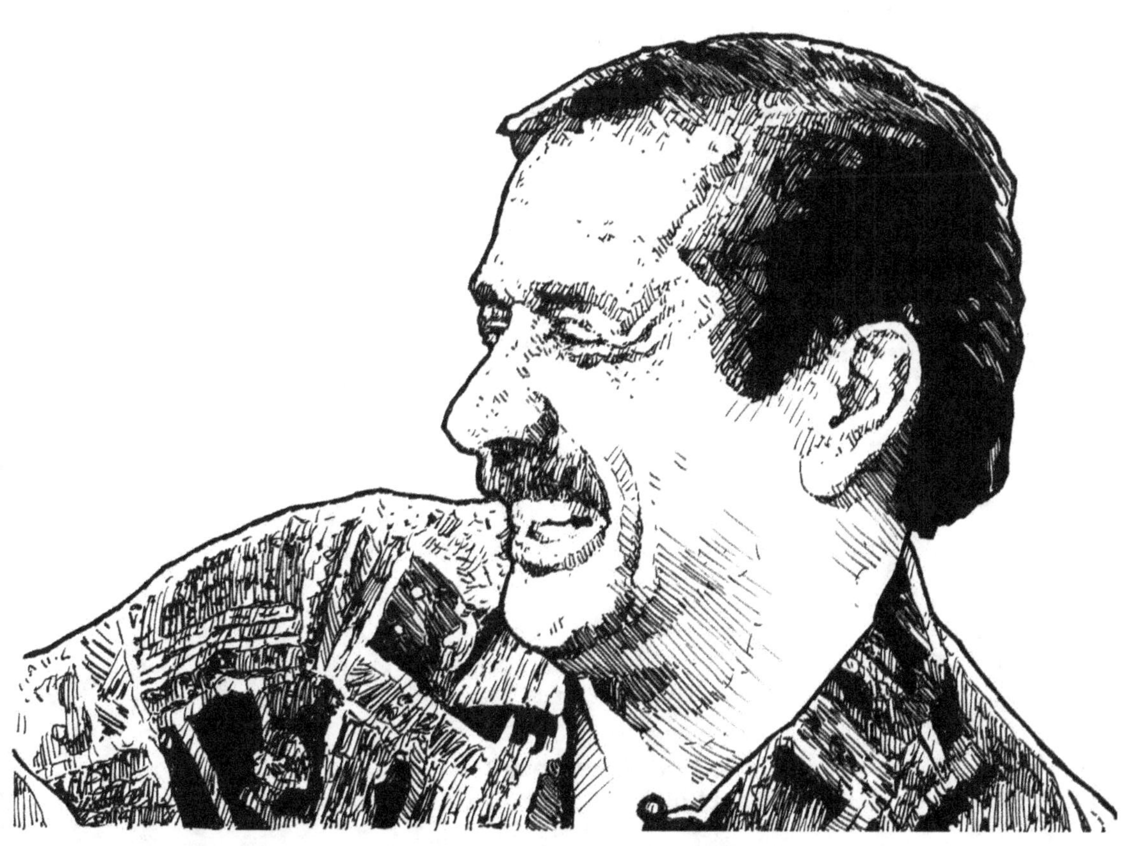

Klaus Kinski (born Klaus Günter Karl Nakszynski)
as Niccolò Paganini, **Paganini** (1989)

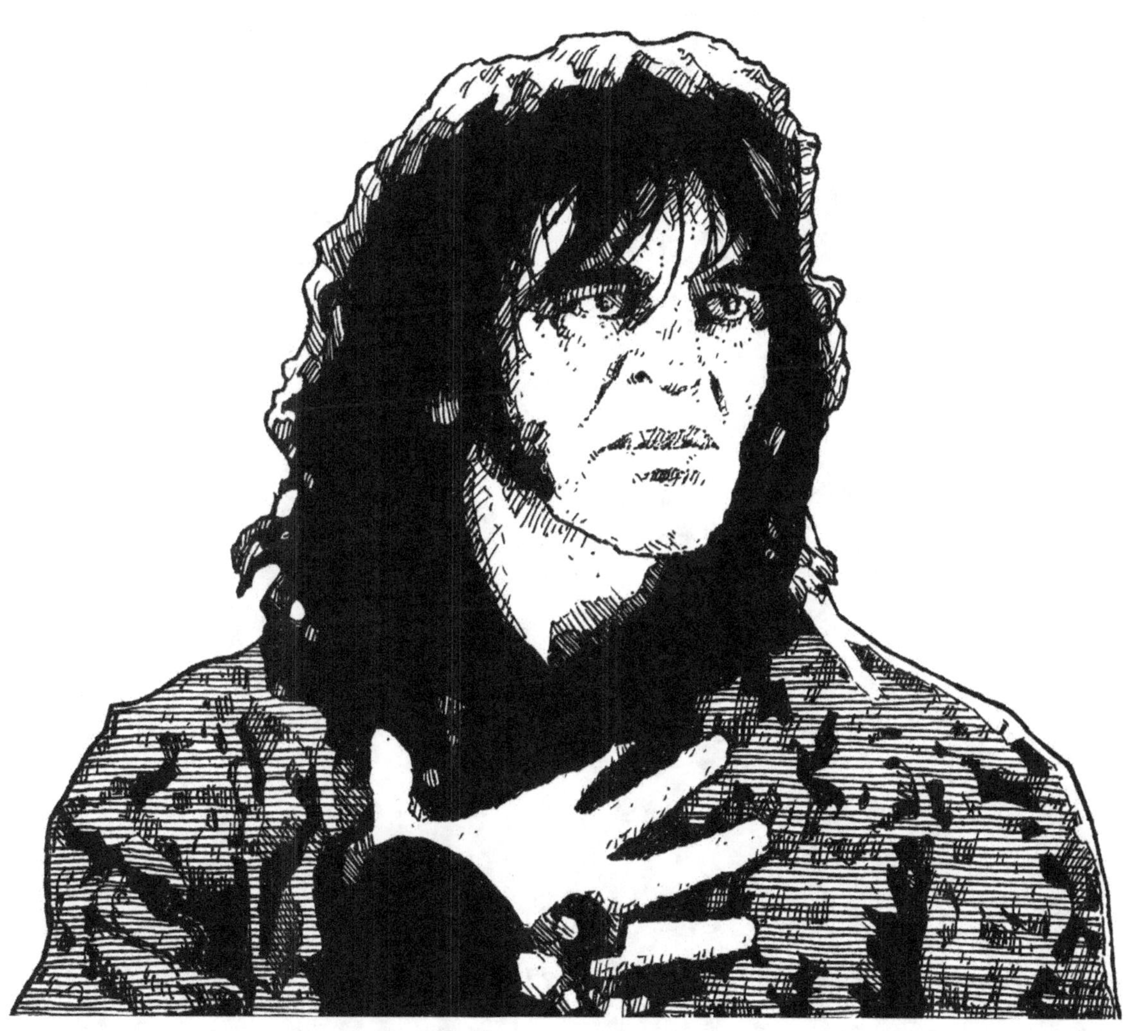

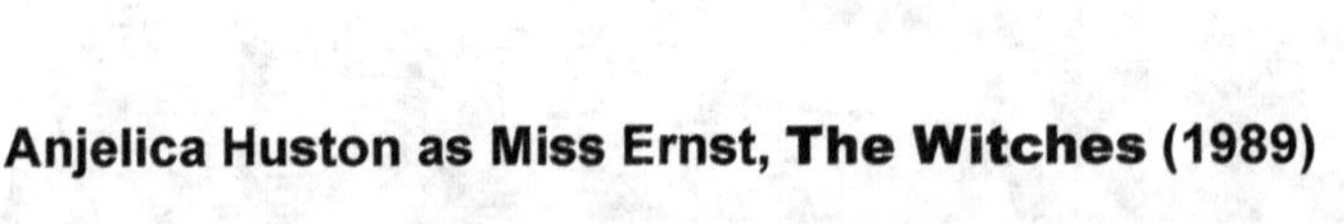
Anjelica Huston as Miss Ernst, *The Witches* (1989)

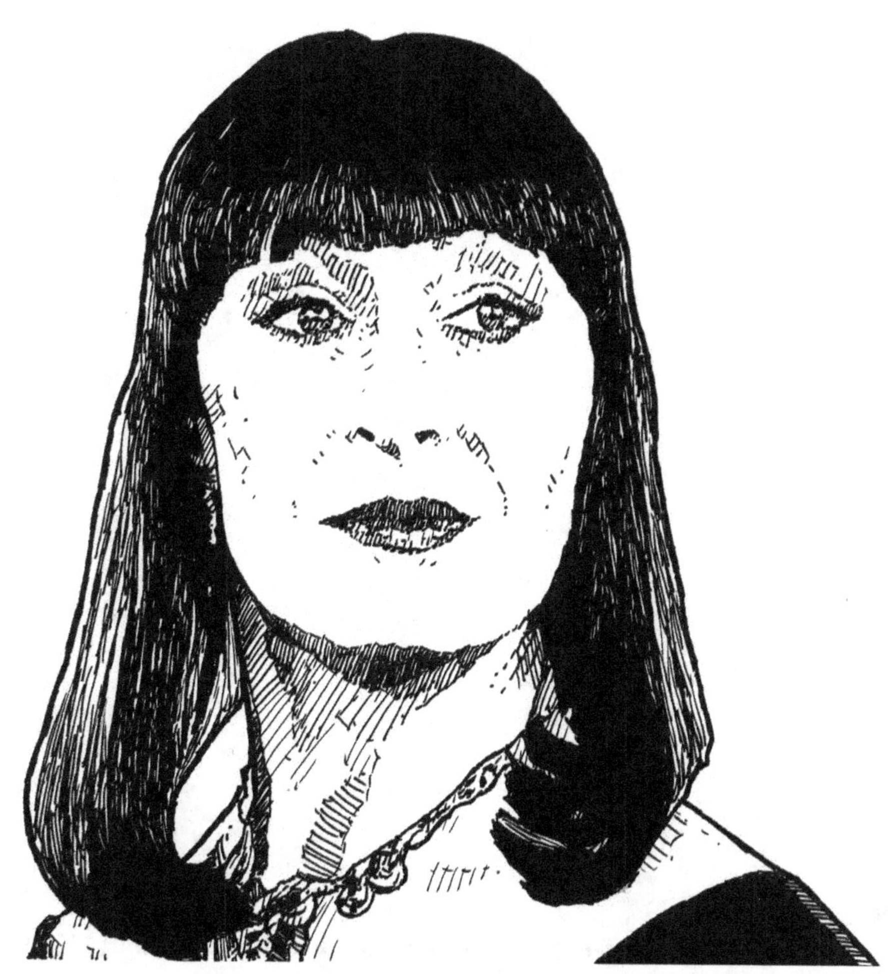

Martin Scorsese
as Vincent Van Gogh, **Dreams [Akira Kurosawa's Dreams]** (1990)

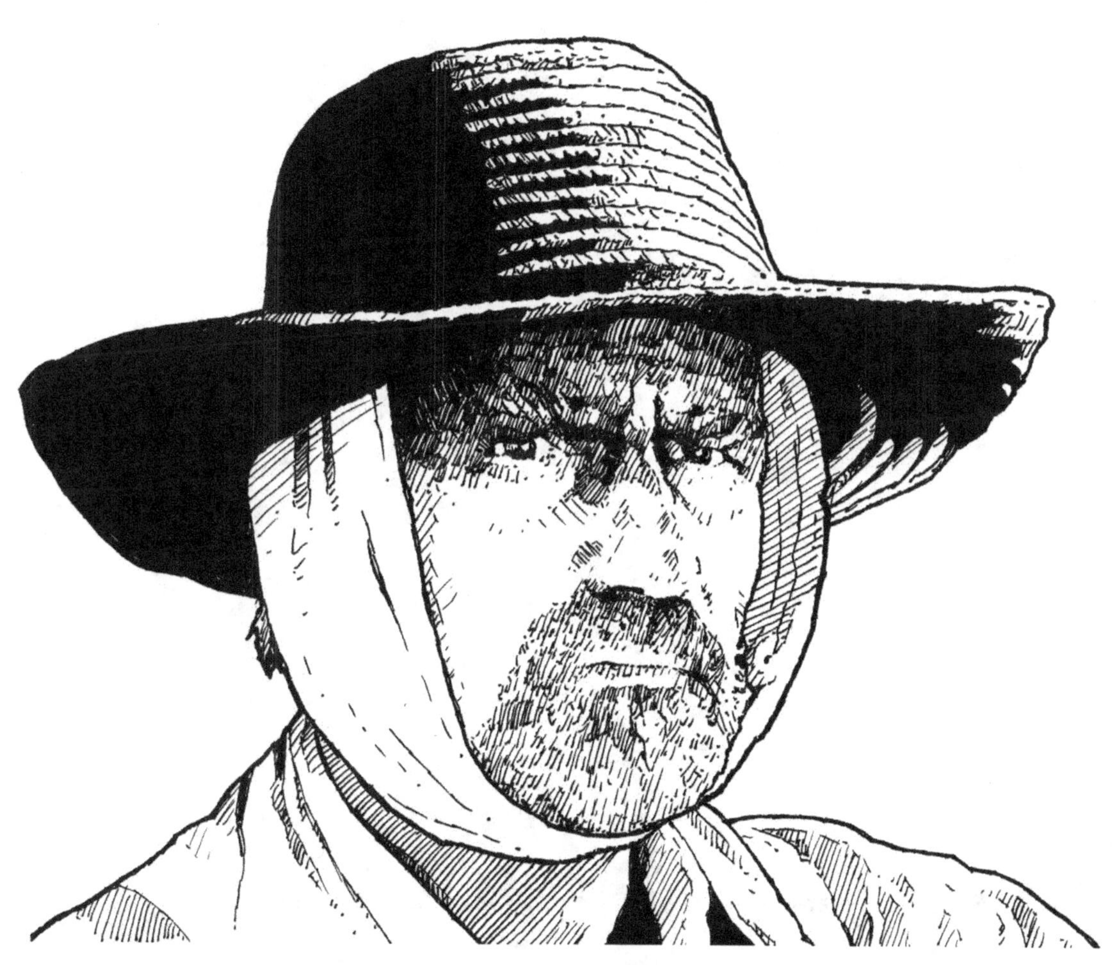

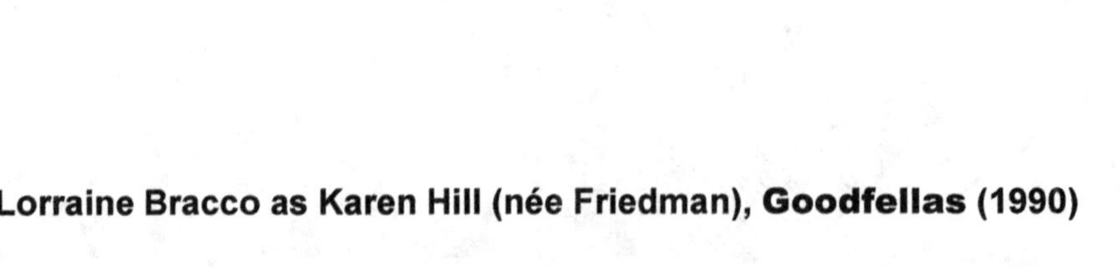

Lorraine Bracco as Karen Hill (née Friedman), Goodfellas (1990)

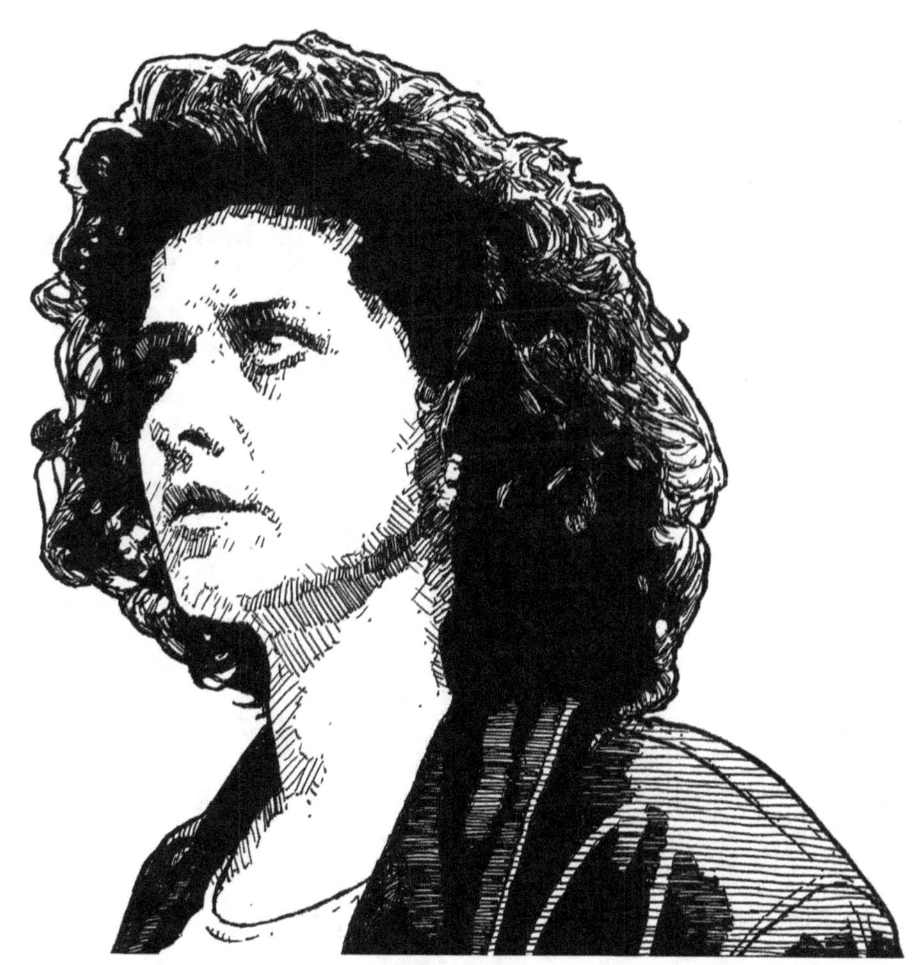

John Turturro as Barton Fink, **Barton Fink** (1991)

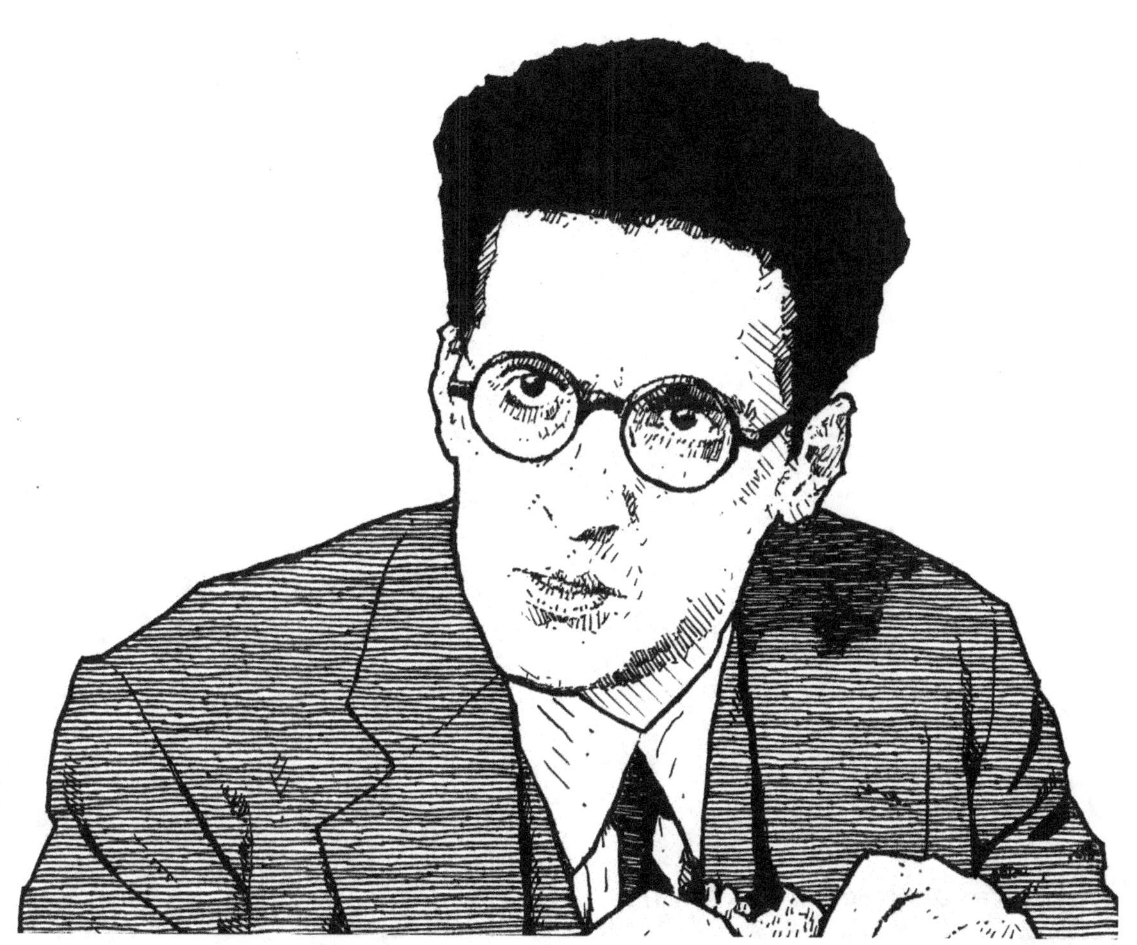

Joe Pesci as David Ferrie, *JFK* (1991)

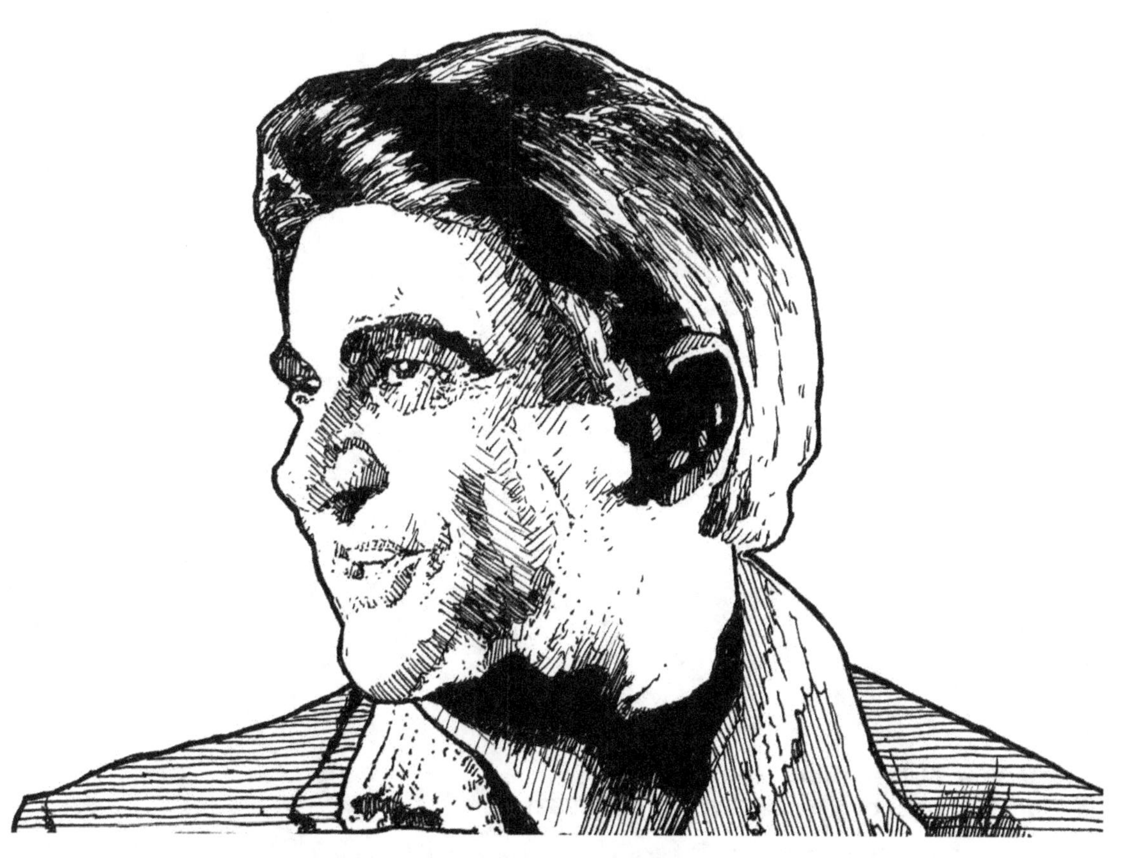

Christopher Walken (born Ronald Walken)
as Vincenzo Coccotti, **True Romance** (1993)

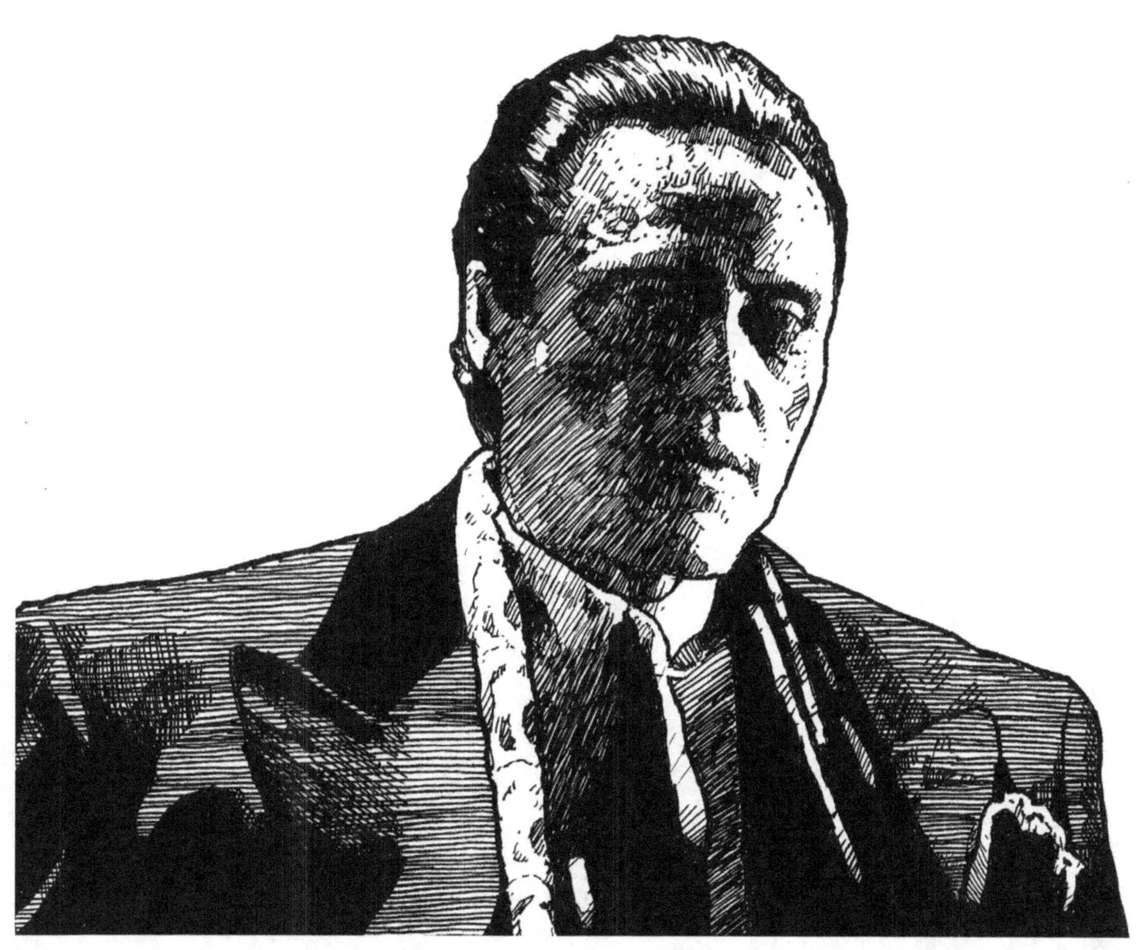

Bob Hoskins as Mario Mario, **Super Mario Bros.** (1993)

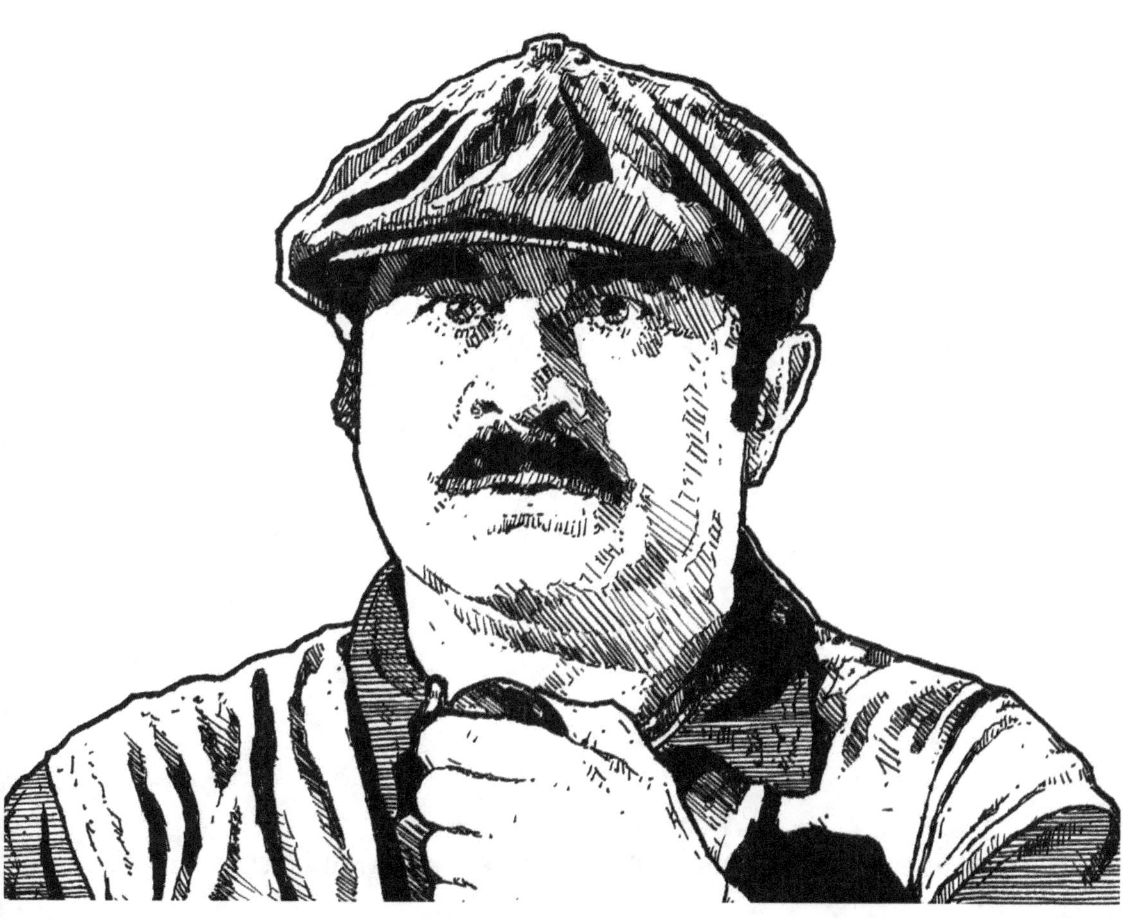

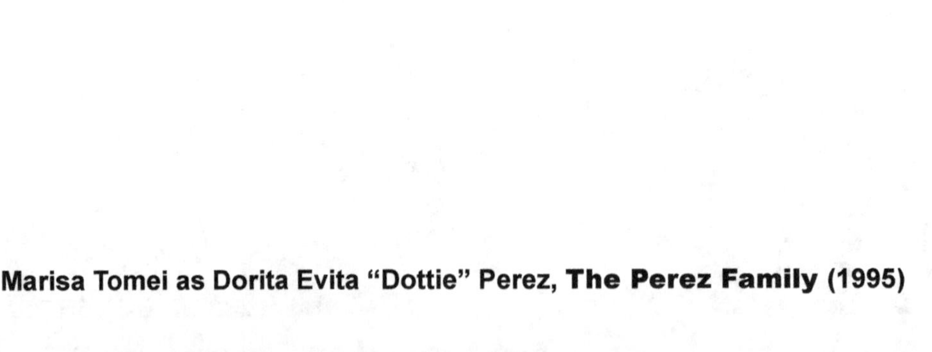

Marisa Tomei as Dorita Evita "Dottie" Perez, **The Perez Family** (1995)

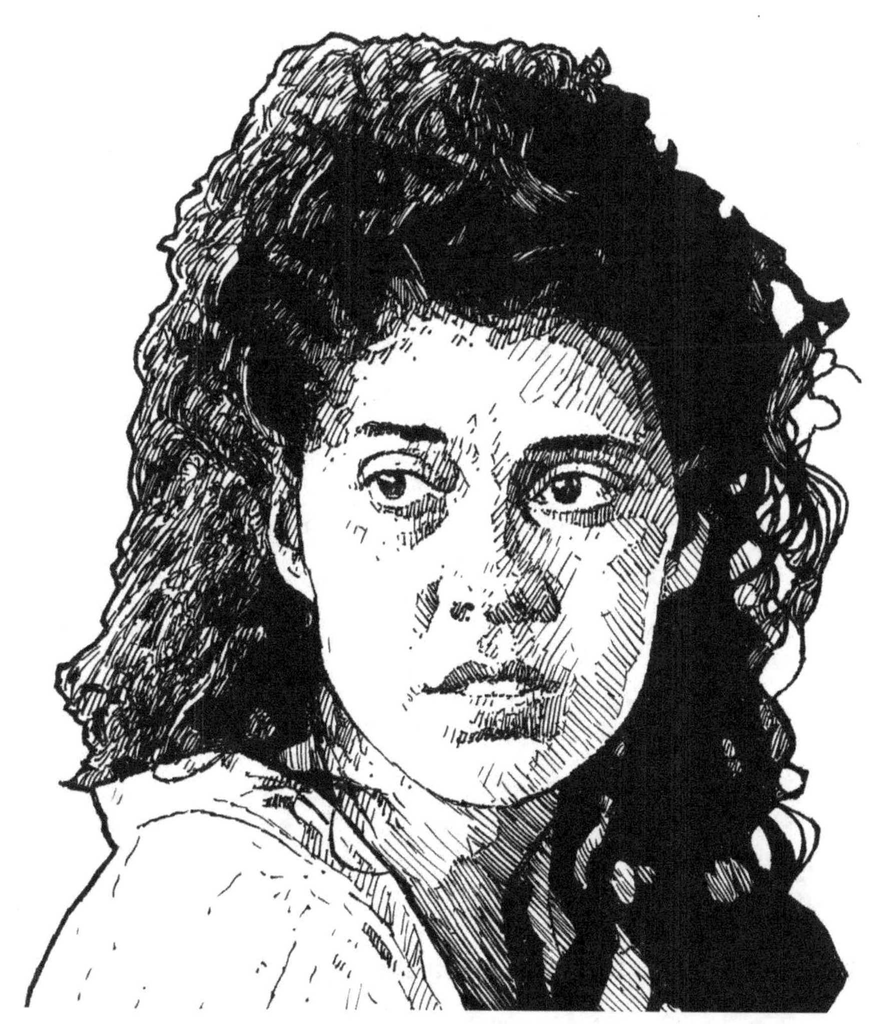

Robert De Niro as Sam "Ace" Rothstein, _Casino_ (1995)

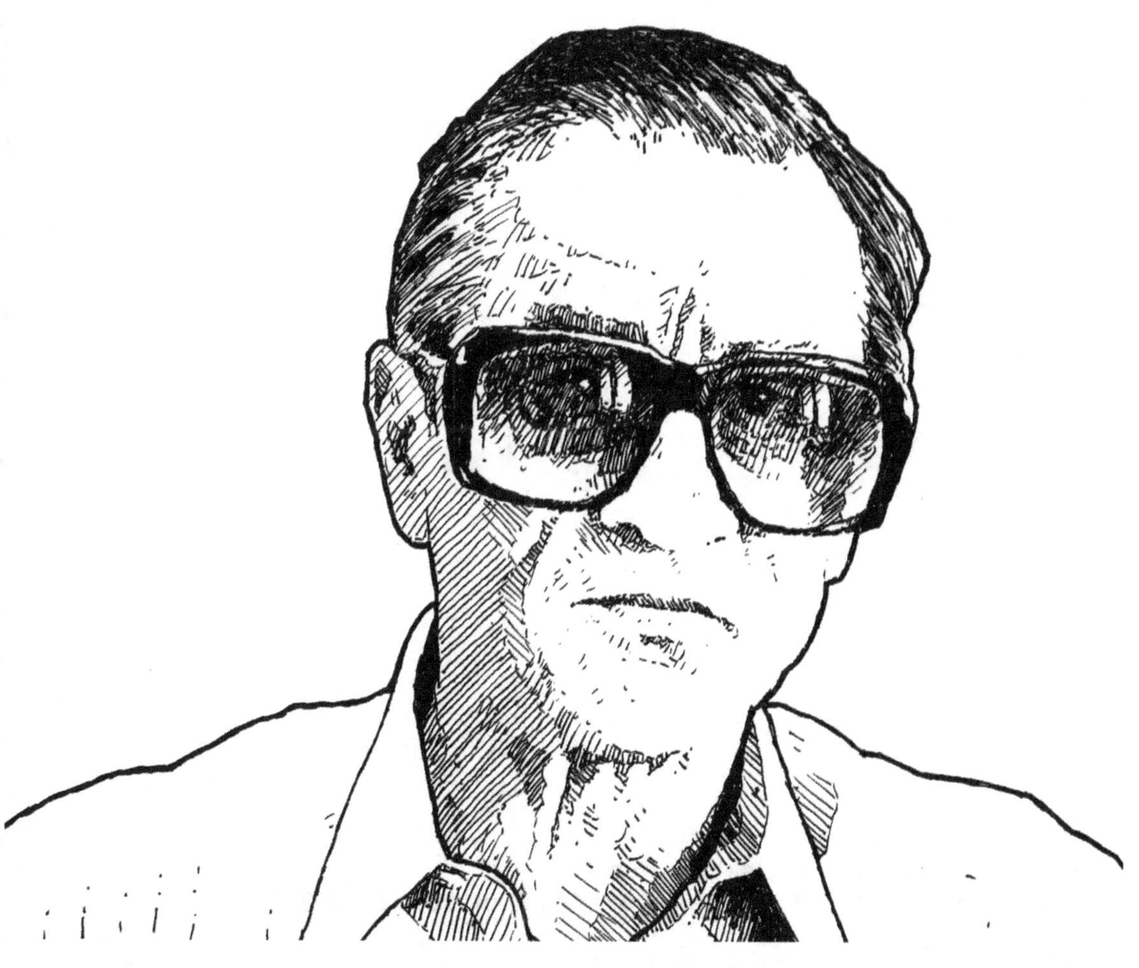

Meryl Streep (born Mary Louise Streep)
as Francesca Johnson, **The Bridges of Madison County** (1995)

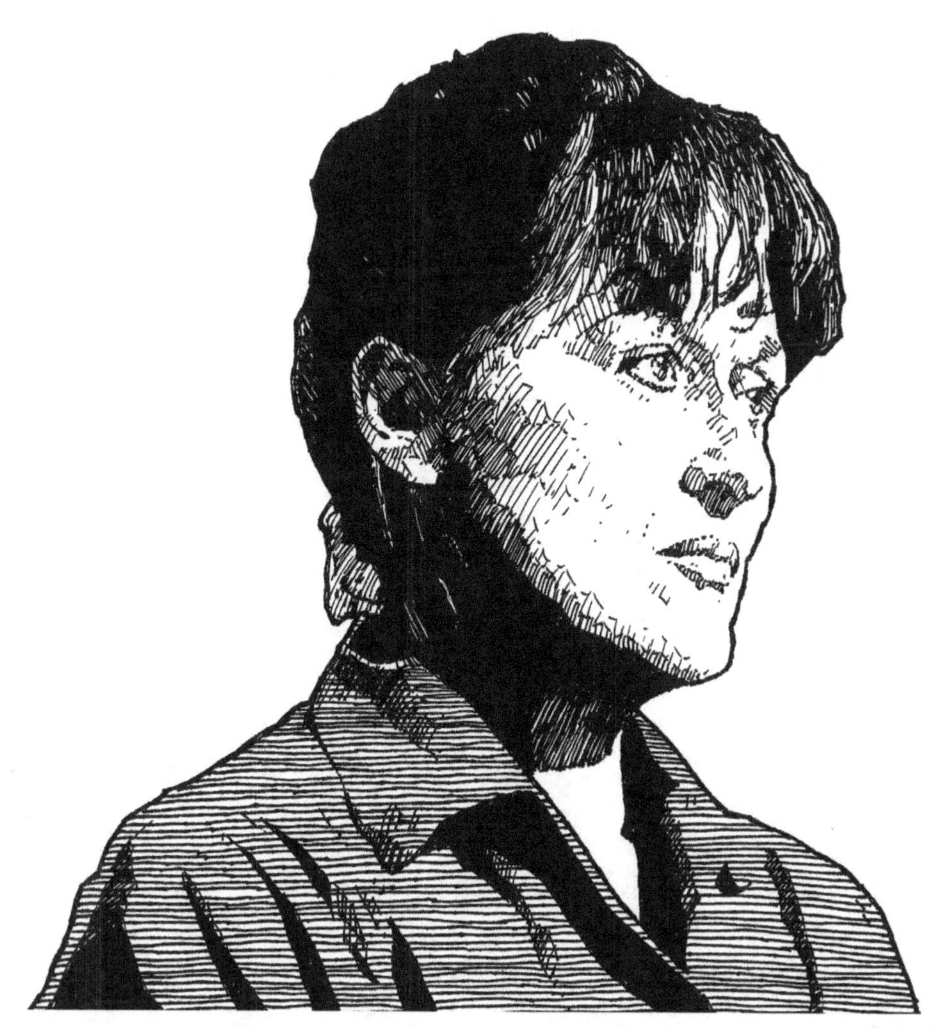

Tony Shalhoub as Primo, **Big Night** (1996)

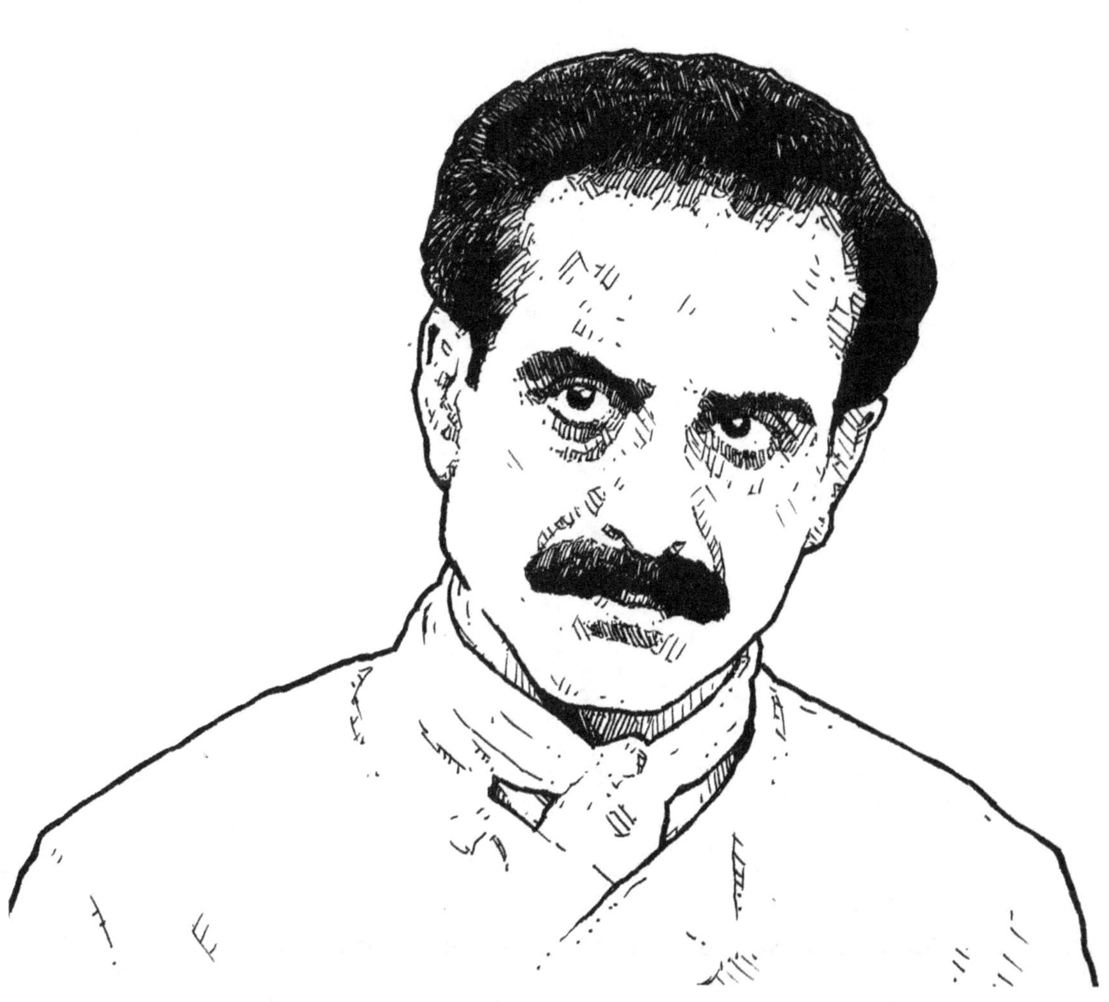

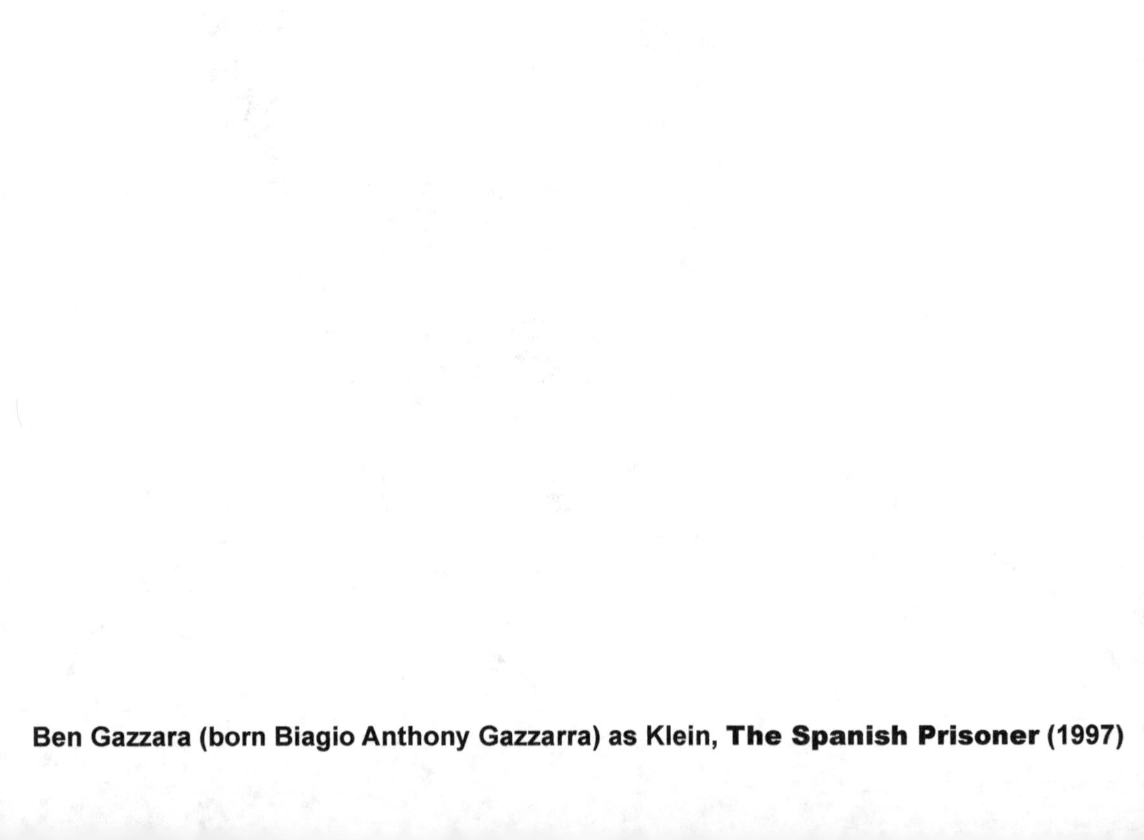

Ben Gazzara (born Biagio Anthony Gazzarra) as Klein, **The Spanish Prisoner** (1997)

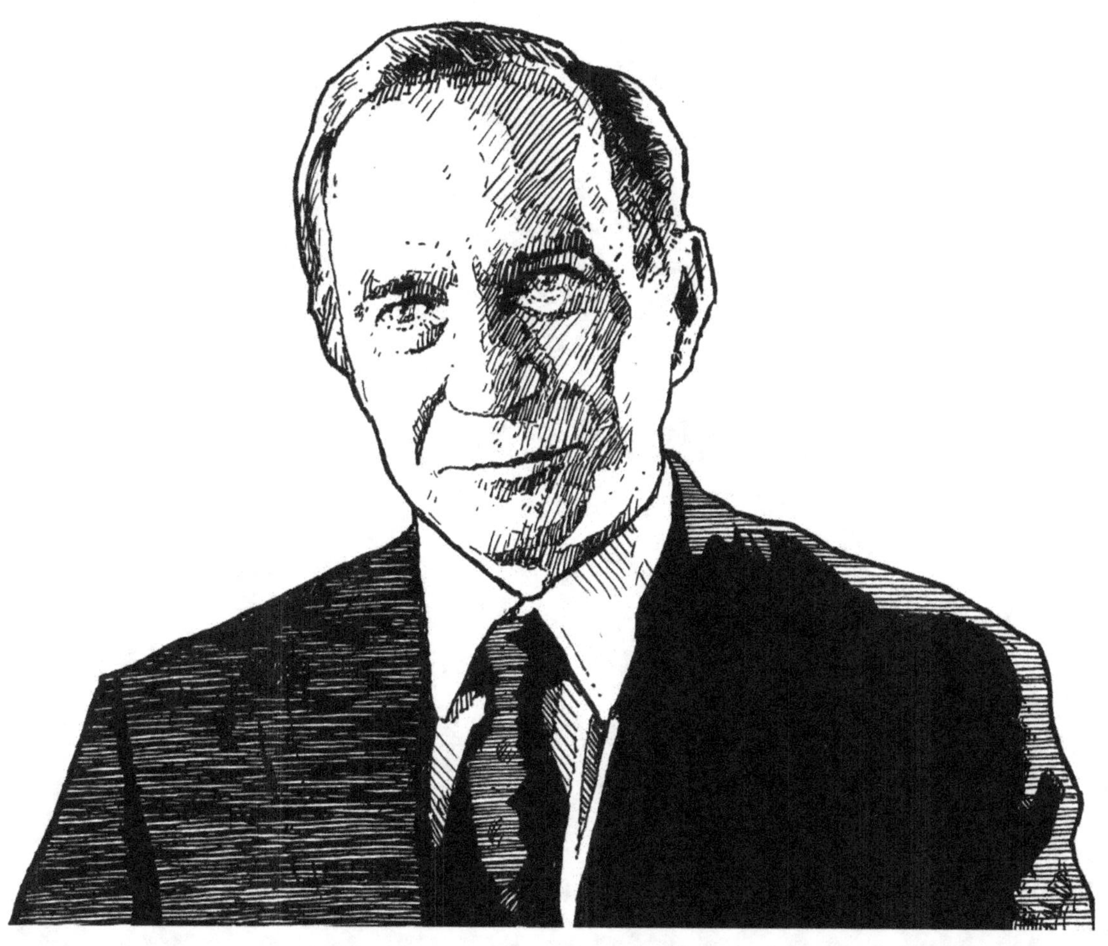

Danny DeVito as Mickey Bergman, Heist (2001)

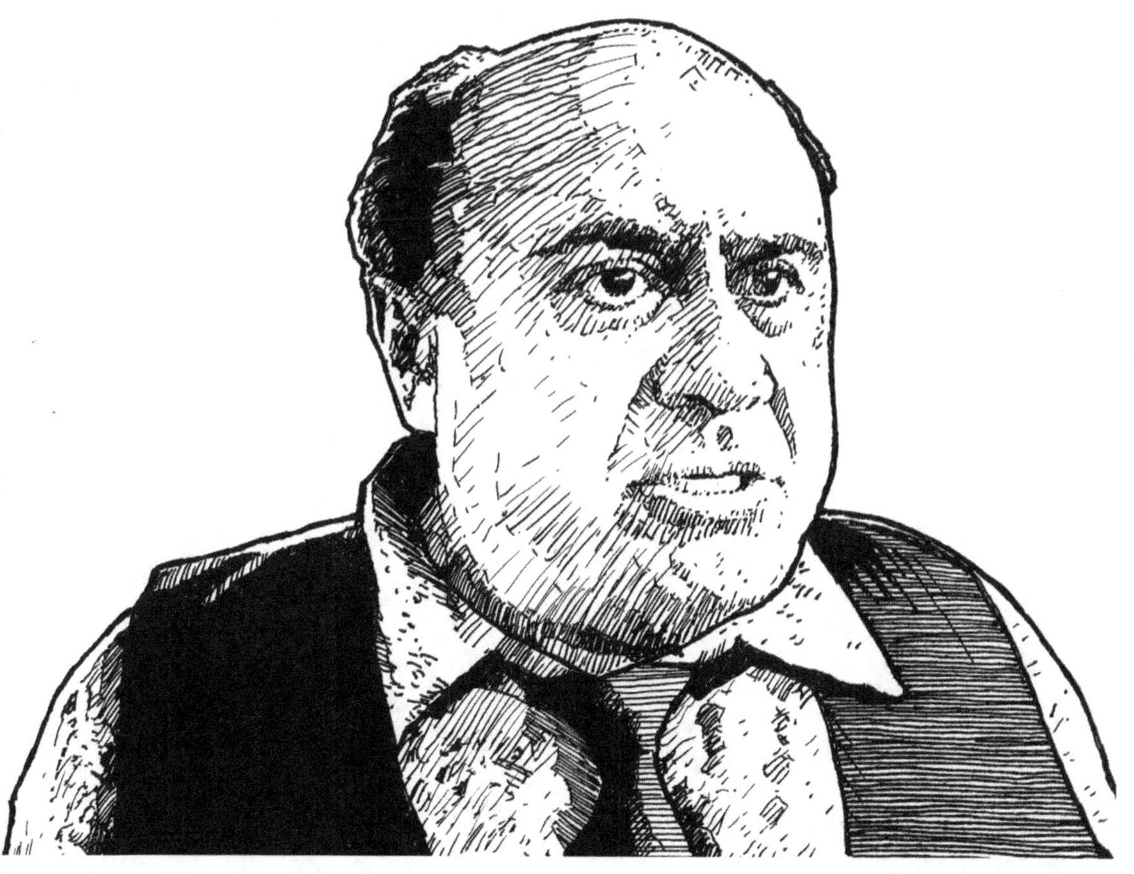

Giancarlo Esposito as Miguel Algarín, **Piñero** (2001)

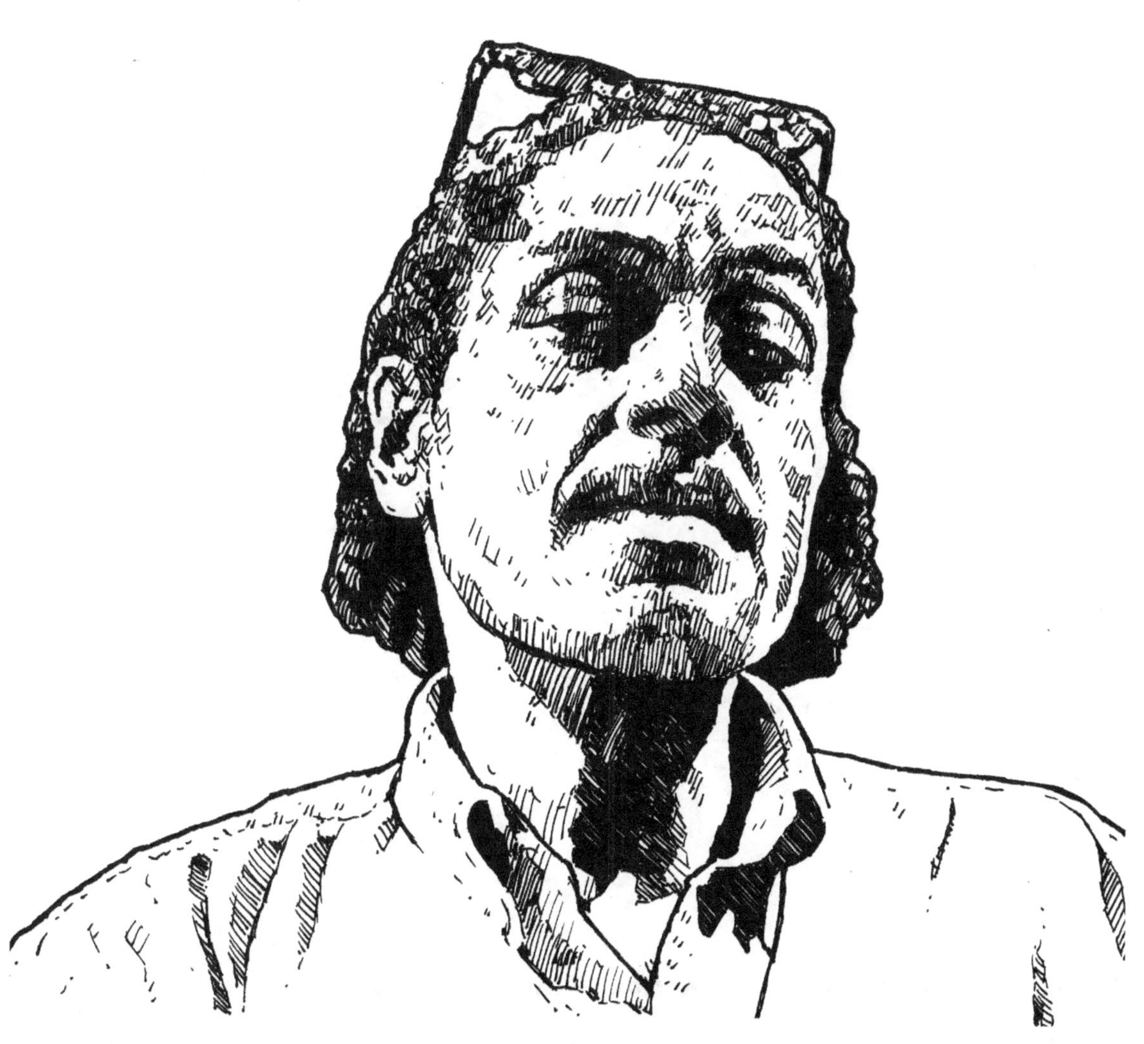

Paul Giamatti as Harvey Pekar, **American Splendor** (2003)

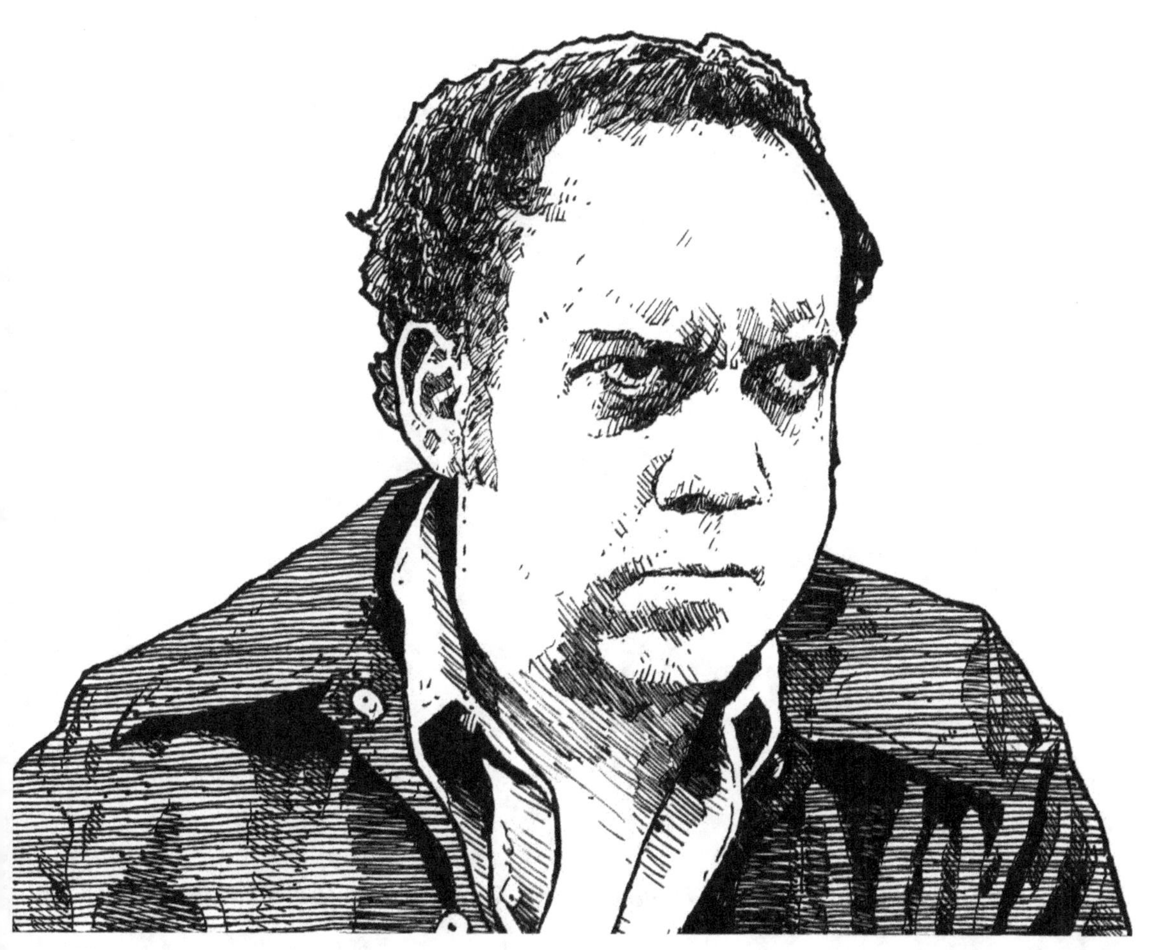

Stanley Tucci as Stanley Kubrick, **The Life and Death of Peter Sellers** (2004)

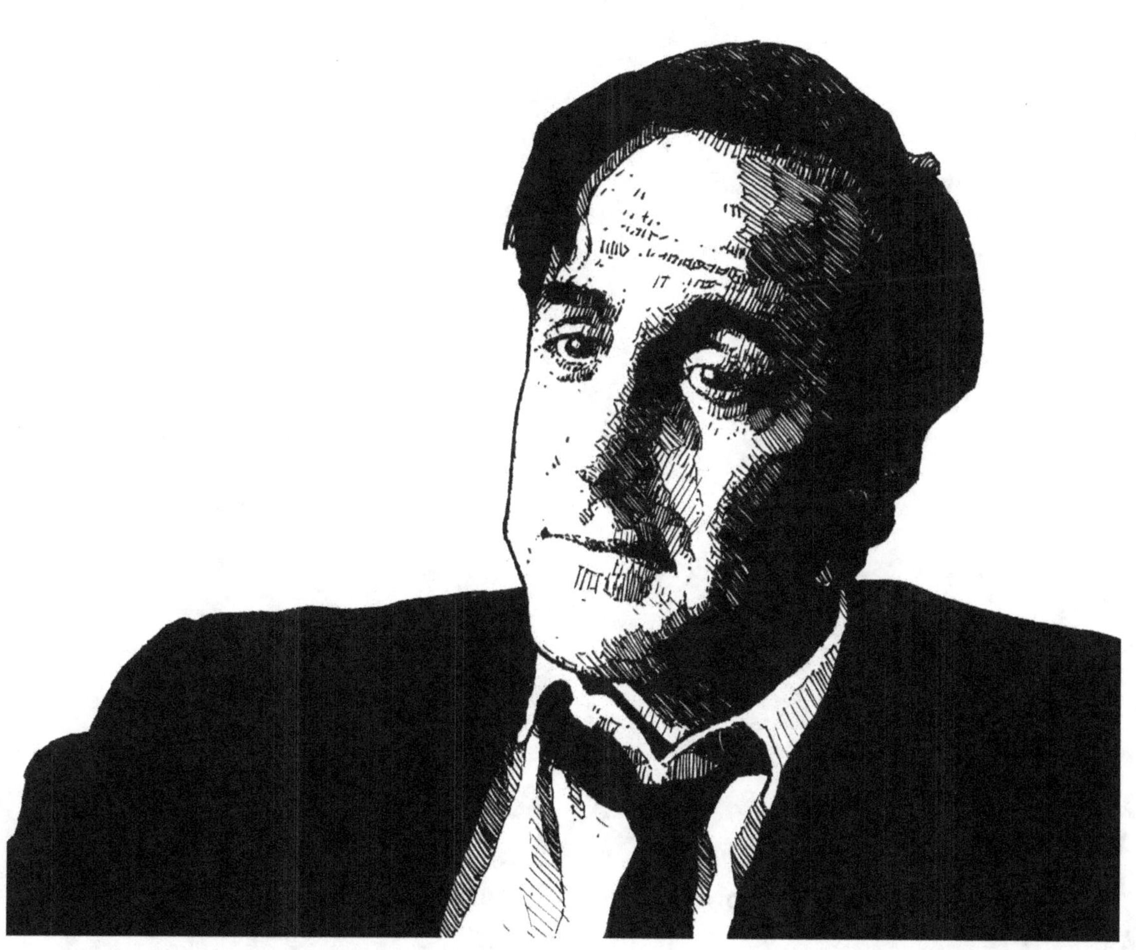

Frank Langella as Richard Nixon, **Frost/Nixon** (2008)

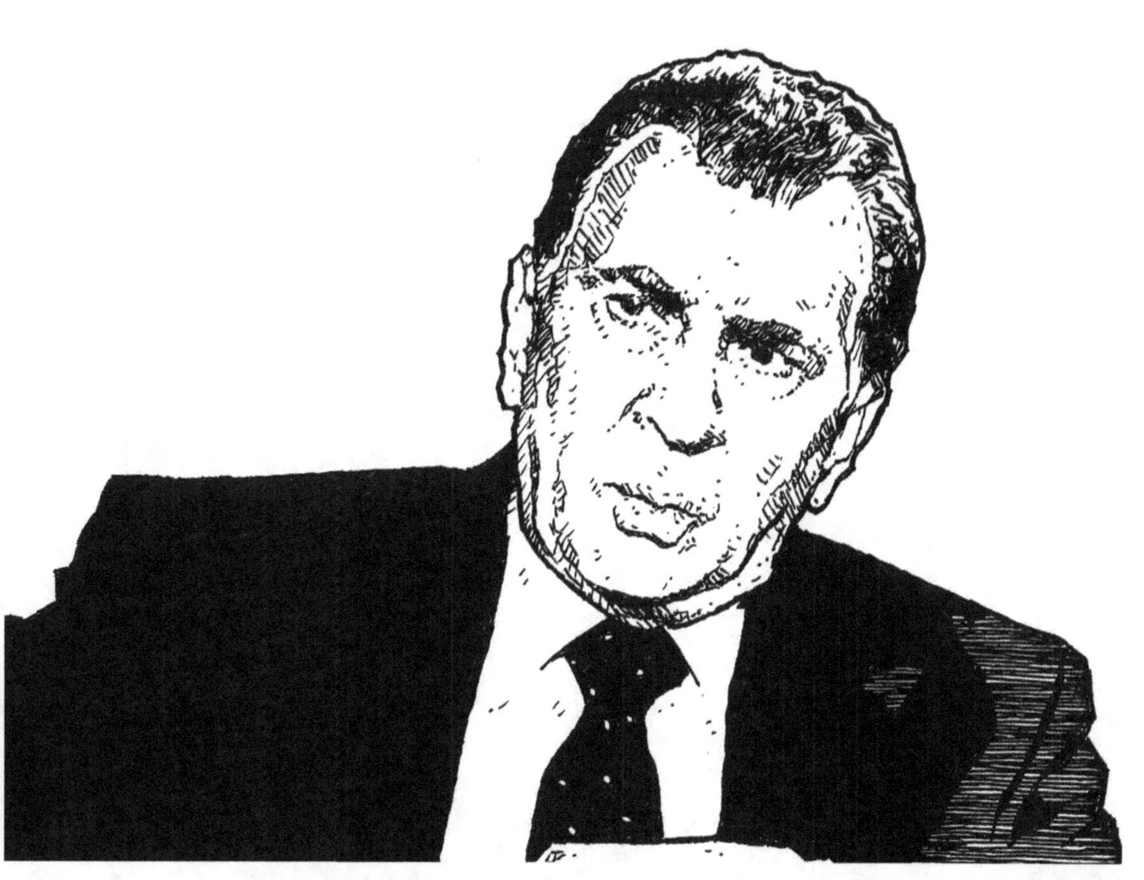

Daniel Day-Lewis as Guido Contini, **Nine** (2009)

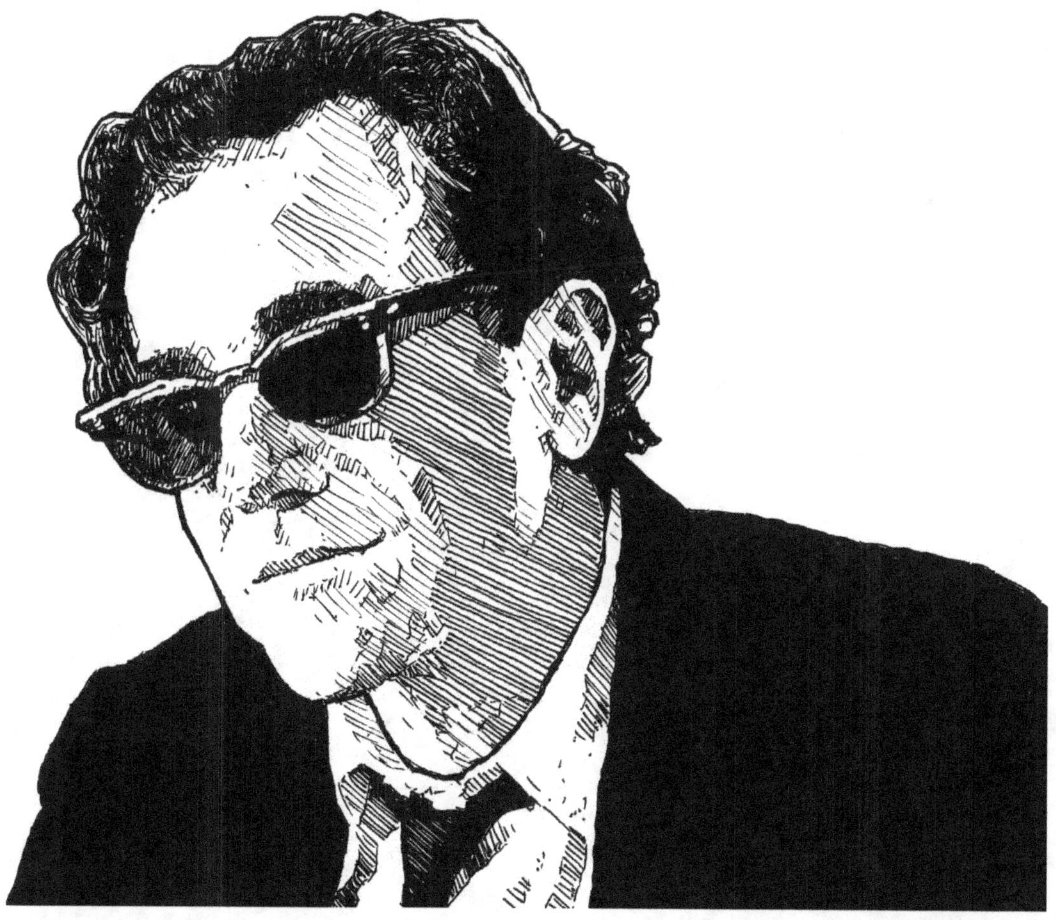

Rene Russo as Frigga, *Thor* (2011)

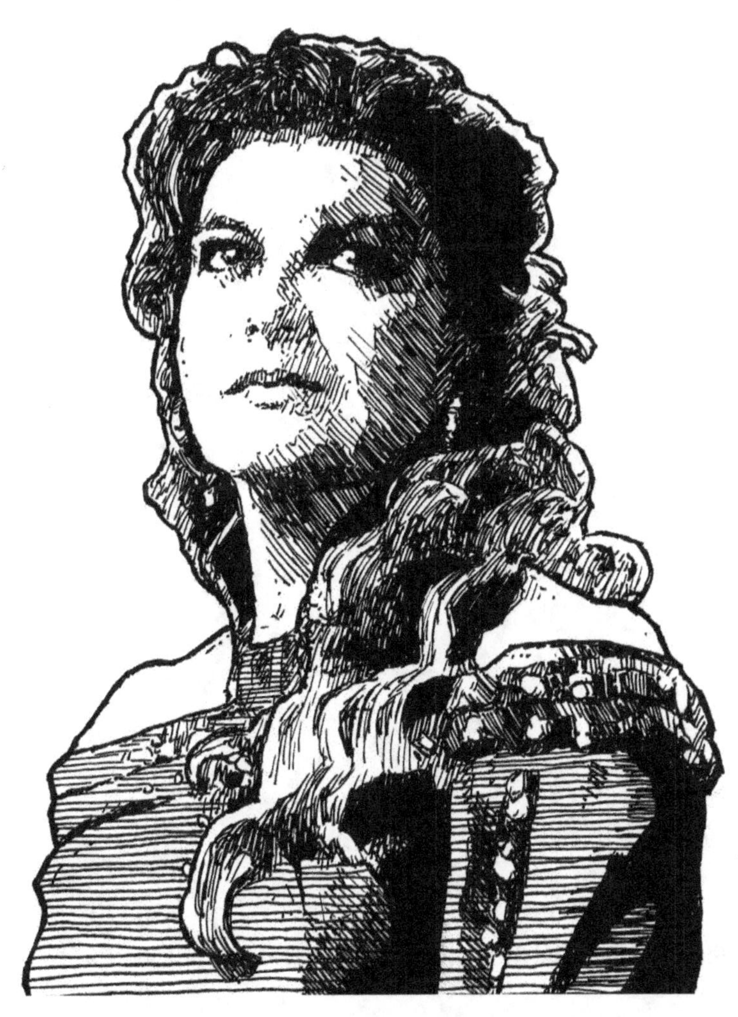

Willem Dafoe (born William James Dafoe) as Pier Paolo Pasolini, **Pasolini** (2014)

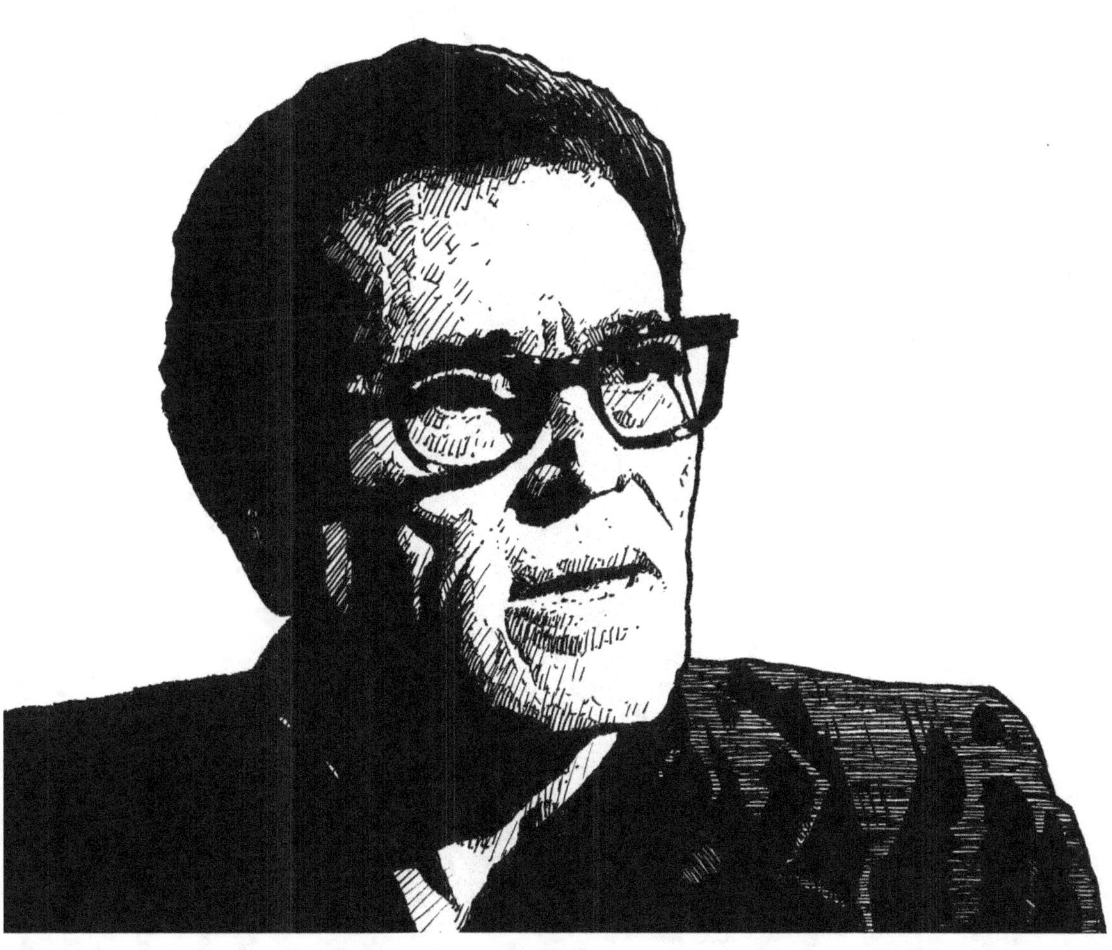

Al Pacino as Jimmy Hoffa, **The Irishman** (2020)

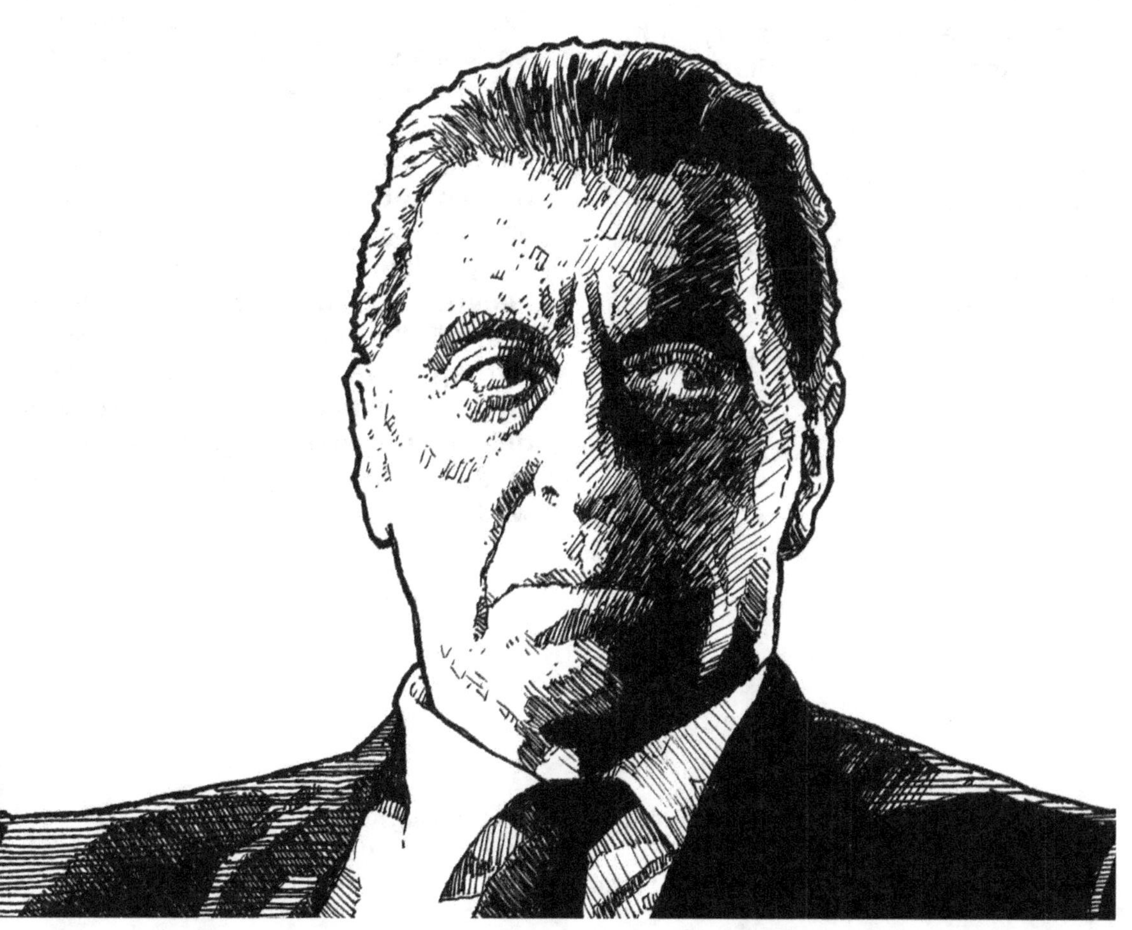

WYATT DOYLE dedicates his work on this project to the memory of his grandfather, a great Italian. Other favorite Italians include Mina, Albert Genna, and Diabolik. He maintains a vibrant and active connection to the old country, primarily via Ennio Morricone records and regular cultural exchanges with Vince at Brothers Pizza. He has published several books. (Wyatt has.)

JIMMY ANGELINA enjoys being Italian, despite being more of a Fredo than a Valentino, and more Afraid-o than Alfredo. Slight joking aside, his favorite thing about being Italian has got to be his Grandma Angelina's otherworldly cooking. All of it was amazing, but he really wishes everybody could have had the opportunity to sample her cheese ravioli; nothing can compare. He has an abiding love for Italian movies, in particular every single thing Federico Fellini ever made. Seeing every Fellini movie at a Film Forum retrospective (**Tutto Fellini**) in New York City when he lived there was one of the best things he ever got to do. He also enjoys gesticulating wildly when roused.

Mickey Rourke (born Philip Andre Rourke, Jr.) as Charlie,
Eric Roberts as Paulie,
The Pope of Greenwich Village (1984)

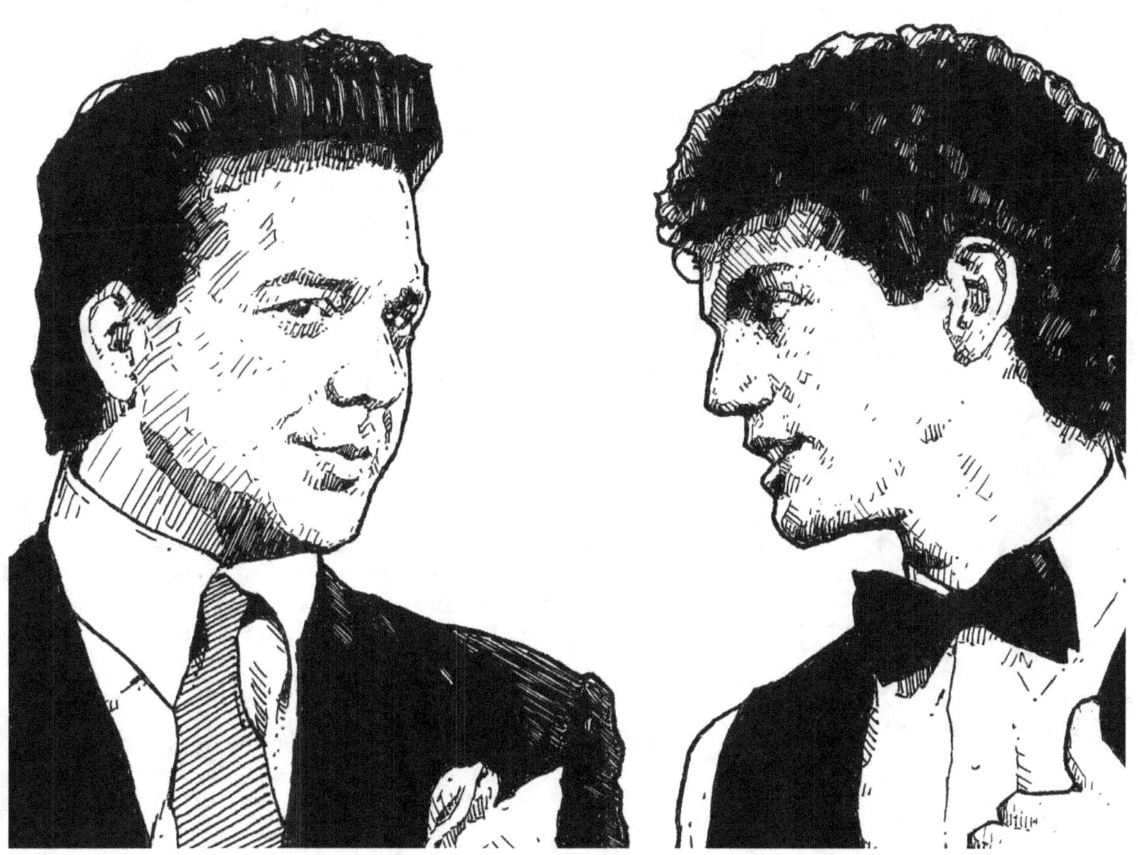

Also from

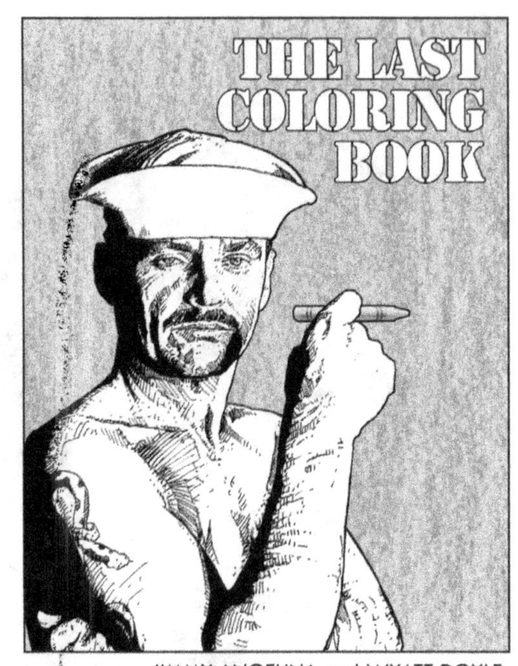

Ceci n'est pas un coloring book

By Jimmy Angelina and Wyatt Doyle
- **The Last Coloring Book**
- **The Last Coloring Book on the Left**

By Wyatt Doyle
- **Stop Requested** illus. Stanley J. Zappa
- **Dollar Halloween**
- **I Need Real Tuxedo and a Top Hat!**
- **Buty-Wave is Now Closed Forever**
- **Jorge Amaya Doesn't Live Here Anymore**

Pop's Cookie Duster
Don & Lee Doyle, illus. Annette Debevec

The Men's Adventure Library
Robert Deis and Wyatt Doyle, series editors
- **Weasels Ripped My Flesh!**
- **He-Men, Bag Men, & Nymphos** Walter Kaylin
- **A Handful of Hell** Robert F. Dorr
- **Cryptozoology Anthology**
- **Barbarians on Bikes**
- **I Watched Them Eat Me Alive**
- **Cuba: Sugar, Sex, and Slaughter**
- **Pollen's Women** Samson Pollen
- **Pollen's Action** Samson Pollen
- **Eva: Men's Adventure Supermodel** Eva Lynd
- **Mort Kunstler: The Godfather of Pulp Illustrators**
- **One Man Army** Gil Cohen
- **Exotic Adventures of Robert Silverberg**
- **Pollen in Print 1958-1959** Samson Pollen
- **Maneaters**

⌗ new texture

By Josh Alan Friedman
- **Black Cracker**
- **Tell the Truth Until They Bleed**

nu luna Andrew Biscontini

By Eric Reymond
- **Nimrodia**
- **Sub-Sub Librarian, Notes on a**

By Richard Adelman
- **Teacher Tales**
- **A Day at the Beach**

By Stanley J. Zappa
The Victorious Triumph of Superior Excellence

Music
- **I've Got Heaven on My Mind**
  Rev. Raymond Branch
- **Sing-Song Songs** Stanley J. Zappa
- **Map of the Moon** s/t
- **Sixty Goddammit** Josh Alan
- **Jimmy Angelina** s/t
- **Cursed** Carolina
- **Continental / International** Jon E. Edwards
- **Live a Little** Manzappaczewski
- **Free / Refuse** Hall, Skrowaczewski, Zappa
- **Crossing Guards** Carter, Leffue, Sikora, Zappa
- **Balloons** Carter, Skrowaczewski, Zappa
- **Turkey Bacon Donuts Bitches**
  MANZAP REBORN
- The Stanley J. Zappa Quartet **Plays for The Society of Women Engineers**

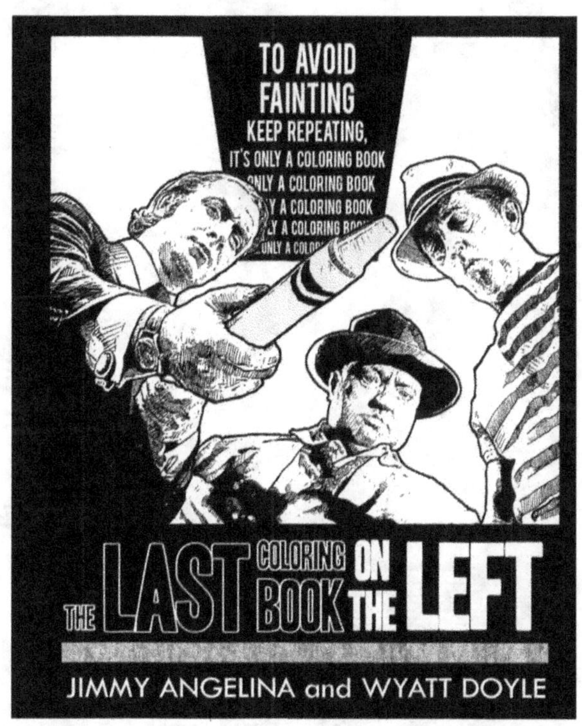

Ceci n'est pas un coloring book non plus [1]

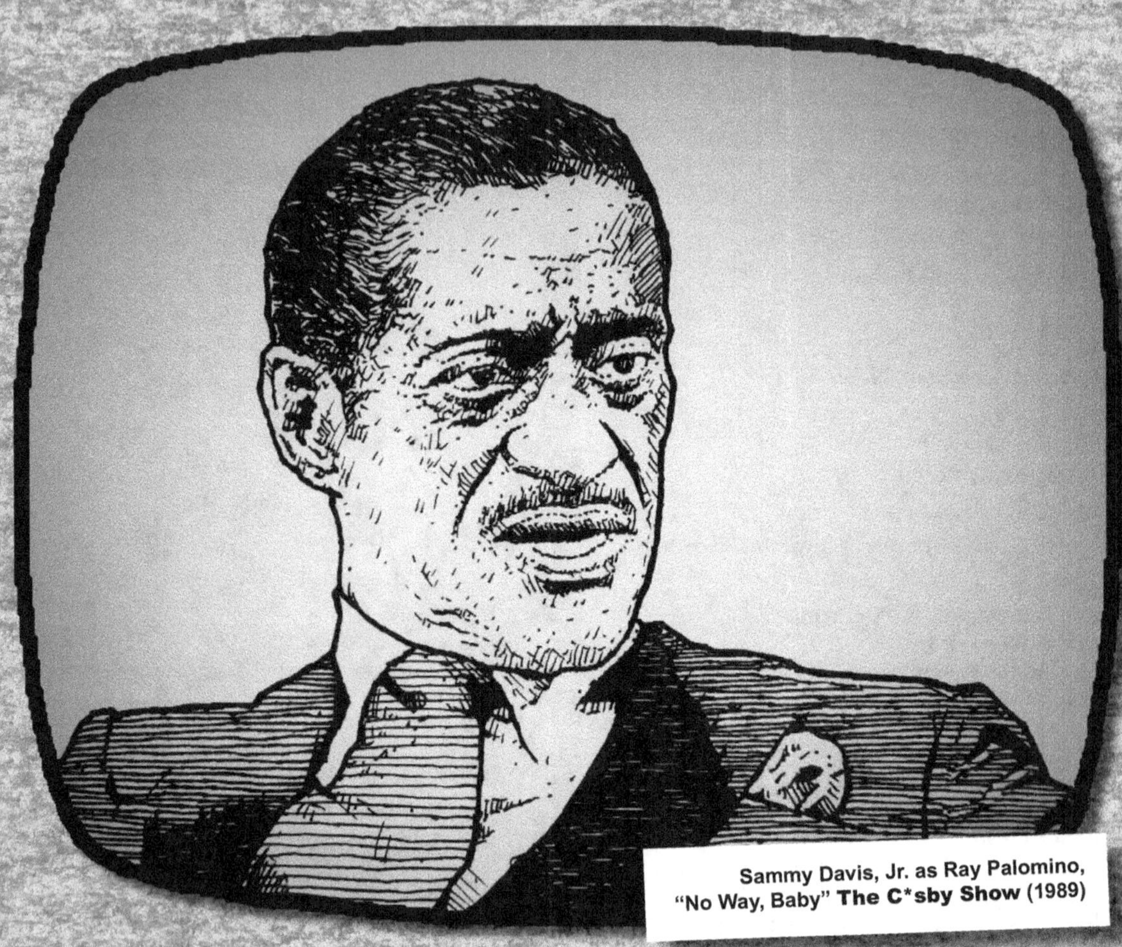

Sammy Davis, Jr. as Ray Palomino,
"No Way, Baby" **The C*sby Show** (1989)

new texture

www.ingramcontent.com/pod-product-compliance
Lightning Source LLC
Chambersburg PA
CBHW080514030726
47592CB00012B/3343